YUCCAS: GIANTS AMONG THE LILIES

by Colin Smith B.Sc. M.Sc.

National Council for the Conservation of Plants & Gardens
Patron: HRH The Prince of Wales

Acknowledgements

I wish to thank:
Caroline, my wife, for her assistance and patience with the writing of this book;
Trevor Key for providing me with some of the references;
Dr. Konrad Näser and Ernst Pagels for their information with regard to Karl Foerster;
Dr. James Cullen for his technical assistance;
Sylvia Norton for her encouragement and assistance;
The NCCPG for their assistance to me as a Collection Holder, and in particular the Nottingham & Derby Committee for their financial support for the printing of this book.

Copyright © Colin Smith B.Sc. M.Sc. 2004.
The moral right of the author has been asserted.
ISBN: 0-9544579-2-7

All rights reserved. No part of this publication may be reproduced, stored in a retrieval system, or transmitted, in any form or by any means, without the prior permission in writing of the publisher, nor be otherwise circulated in any form of binding or cover other than that in which it is published and without a similar condition including this condition being imposed on the subsequent purchaser.

Designed and produced by Gilmour Print   www.gilmourprint.co.uk
Published by The National Council for the Conservation of Plants and Gardens   www.nccpg.com

Trevor Key showing the Renishaw Hall National Collection of Yuccas for NCCPG members.

Contents

Introduction	4
General Information	4
Historic Economic Uses	5
Modern Economic Uses	6
Cultivation	7
Propagation	8
Pests and Diseases	8
Catalogue and Key to Subgenera	9
Subgenus Yucca	10
Subgenus Clistocarpa	31
Subgenus Chaenocarpa	33
Subgenus Hesperoyucca	57
Hybrids	61
Appendix I: Hardy Species	63
Appendix II: Breeders and Cultivars	64
Appendix III: Where to obtain and where to see yuccas	67
Appendix IV: Glossary	68
Bibliography	69
Index	71

Introduction

I started acquiring yuccas in 1988 and was granted NCCPG National Collection status in 1993. The collection now has about one hundred taxa, predominantly the hardier species and cultivars, but also a limited number of the more tender species. The tender ones are maintained in pots and kept under glass, frost free in a standard domestic greenhouse and lean-to glasshouse of similar size. During the summer months some are relocated into the garden.

The soil here in Burwell, Cambridgeshire is alkaline; two thirds of a metre down it is solid chalk, locally known as clunch. Our rainfall is about 50cm per year. Frosts can occur reliably between November and April, sometimes May. Snowfall has never exceeded 10cm in the last ten years, however the winter of 2000-2001 with its exceptional rainfall has been more damaging than usual.

General Information

The name *Yucca* was applied to the genus by Gerard, who in error had derived it from the word 'Yuca', the Carib Indian name for the unrelated crop plant, cassava, *Manihot esculenta*.

Yuccas in fact belong to the family *Agavaceae*. This once included the *Agaveae, Dracaeneae, Nolineae, Phormieae* and *Polyantheae*. In 1985, however, Dahlgren, Clifford and Yeo undertook a revision of the monocotyledons, restricting the *Agavaceae* family to closely related genera from the Americas only. These are: *Agave, Beschorneria, Fourcraea, Hesperaloe, Manfreda, Polianthes, Prochnyanthes* and *Yucca*.

The genus originates exclusively from the New World. Species occur from Canada and the United States of America, through Mexico, into Central America and the Caribbean. Over this range, they are to be found in a range of habitats, including the Great Plains, the Rocky and Appalachian Mountains, the coastal dunes of the Atlantic and Gulf of Mexico, the deserts of the USA and Mexico and the tropical rainforests of Central America and the Caribbean.

The species vary from stem-less clumps to small trees. There is even an exceptional epiphytic species. The leaves may be thick and rigid to thin and flexible. Leaf margins may be denticulate or with curly fibres. The very showy flowers are white but may be shaded cream or violet and cup or saucer shaped. The flowers, normally pendent, are usually borne on upright panicles. The flowers open at night, because their pollination is carried out by small moths of the genus *Tegeticula*; these occur throughout the yuccas' natural range. The moths deliberately gather a ball of pollen, which they thrust down into the stigmatic chamber. At the same time they lay their eggs, the larvae then feeding exclusively on the maturing seeds. This is the reason why in the United Kingdom with two notable exceptions, yuccas do not set seed.

There are in the genus *Yucca* over fifty species and at least as many again described subspecies and forms. In addition there are at least one hundred and fifty cultivars and hybrids, many of which are probably no longer extant.

The first yuccas to be introduced into Britain were those from the eastern seaboard of what became the United States of America. The initial introductions were *Yucca gloriosa* (1596) and *Yucca aloifolia* (1605). To put this into historical context, the first permanent English colony, Jamestown, Virginia, was not established until 1607. Subsequent early introductions include *Yucca filamentosa* (1675), *Yucca recurvifolia* (1794) and *Yucca flaccida* (1816). Most of the garden varieties are derived from these species.

Historic Economic Uses

The American Indians of the South Western United States have, since prehistoric times, made extensive use of yuccas for a wide variety of purposes. This more arid region has a great diversity and concentration of these plants and therefore they are an important natural resource in this harsh environment.

The use of yuccas as a food is known to have occurred widely and for a considerable time. Exploration of the prehistoric ruins of Bee Cave Canyon, Texas, produced the remains of yucca pods and seeds. These were identified as *Yucca thompsoniana*, *Yucca elata* and *Yucca torreyi*. It is, however, *Yucca baccata*, with its large banana-like fruit, which was mostly prized. Frequently it was collected while still green, to ripen safely away from wild animals, which would also enjoy it. The fruit was either eaten raw or cooked. The pulp was often dried and stored for later use. When cooked, it would produce thick syrup that was consumed as a sweet beverage or as a sauce-like desert.

The Zuni Indians would gather the unripe fruits of *Yucca glauca*, which they would boil to make a sweet pickle. However, this would never be eaten with other foods, as they thought to do so would give them stomach disorders.

The seeds of yuccas were also collected and stored, to be ground into meal as required.

The Apache Indians would gather the crowns of *Yucca elata*, from Spring to Summer, cooking them over night. They can then be sun-dried; the resultant product could then be broken into pieces, softened in water and eaten. The large flowers were boiled and eaten as a vegetable.

The Indians found the greatest use for yuccas was for cordage, dating as far back as prehistoric times. Archaeological finds show every stage of production, from sheaves of whole leaves through chewed or pounded leaves and hanks of cleaned fibre, to the finished product. Yucca string was stout and compared well with modern counterparts. The twine was used for many purposes: fastening matting and latticework in cradles, netting bags, tying materials, fixing feather work for ceremonial paraphernalia and lashing flint points to arrows.

There were also sandals made from yucca leaves. These could involve weaving the actual leaf, or they could be woven from yucca cord. This, however, did involve a tremendous amount of work.

The Navajo Indians also made extensive use of yuccas for producing basketwork. The most important use was for ceremonial drums in their ancient rites, when a regular drum would never be used. The drumstick was even formed from the stout leaf of *Yucca baccata*.

The Apache used yucca leaves widely in their basketry, particularly *Yucca baccata*, *Yucca torreyi* and *Yucca elata*. They produced geometric designs by incorporating the red of yucca roots and the white of the interior of the leaves. Sometimes the baskets may have been sealed with pitch applied from a fibre brush.

The Zuni Indians would split the leaves of *Yucca baccata* to weave into mats to cover grain vases and other vessels. In prehistoric times yucca-leaf wicker mats were used in burying the dead. Bedding mats were made by inter weaving yucca leaves and the inner bark of willow.

The roots of yuccas were prized for their high content of saponin, which was used as soap by some Indians. The roots were washed and crushed; this could then be applied directly to the hair, or allowed to soak in water, in which case the soapy liquid was used.

The Zuni would also weave skirts and kilts from yucca leaves, before the introduction of sheep. Zuni legend has it that the first garments they made upon emerging from the underworld were made from yuccas.

Tewa Indians would make fishing nets from yucca leaves, which they would stretch across a river. The bottom was weighted with stones and the top was kept up by tying on gourds as floats.

Modern Economic Uses

The ability of yuccas to survive in harsh desert environments means that they can be used to assist in stabilizing sands and to counter erosion. They can also, by adding organic matter, increase water retention in the soil and increase its fertility. Because of these properties their potential use has been researched in many countries, including the Republics of Uzbekistan and Turkmenistan.

Yuccas provide food and shelter for wildlife and livestock alike. In the United States they have been used as a cattle feed during drought years. The leaves are chopped up for silage and mixed with concentrates made from seed meal. In Mexico they have been planted to form dense impenetrable hedges, ideal as corrals.

In recent times yucca juice has proved to be of great value as a base in liquid fertilizers. It has the ability to reduce the surface tension of irrigation water, and greatly enhance the ability of the water to penetrate heavy soil. It assists soil flocculation, and provides a good carrying agent for plant nutrients. The yucca extract is itself rich in trace elements, which include boron, iron, magnesium, manganese, copper and zinc.

Another use for the juice is as a carbon dioxide stabilizer in the control of oil fires. Also the saponin from yuccas is considered a good base for soaps, cleansing powders and toothpaste. It has been found that yucca rhizomes provide a rich source of the female hormone desorycorticorcerone, valuable in gynaecological work. Also it has been suggested that the leaves of *Yucca elephantipes* could be a potential commercial source of ascorbic acid.

The most extensive use of yuccas has been the production of fibre. Although in the United

States other sources of twine have been preferred, in Mexico fibre production has been considerable In the States of Zacateca and San Luis Potosi, production in 1964, was as high as 6000 tons; at this time the peasants largely responsible for its production used yucca trunks to build the walls of their huts, and yucca leaves to cover their roofs. Since then, out put has been reduced.

In the United States, yuccas were used in the manufacture of paper during the Second World War. Today, yucca wood is used there to produce panels for covering walls. These are ornamental but also good insulators against both temperature and sound.

Various plants of this genus are used ornamentally in parks and gardens, throughout the Americas and Europe. *Yucca elephantipes* is not only a familiar houseplant, but also widely used by tropical plant hire companies for foyer displays and the like. In Mexico, *Yucca filifera* and *Yucca carnerosana* have been planted beside some roads, not only for aesthetic reasons, but also to assist their consolidation.

Yuccas are still widely used for food in Central America. In Mexico the fruits of several species, wrongly named as 'datiles' or 'dates' are eaten. The flowers are also eaten, fresh or canned. In Guatemala and Costa Rica the blooms of *Yucca elephantipes* are used as vegetables, as are the 'hearts', i.e. the tender inner part of the base of new leaves.

Cultivation

The most important rule when growing all species of yucca is that they hate wet feet. Although they can tolerate a generous amount of rain, it must be able to drain quickly from the roots.

Hardy Species

The hardy species do not seem concerned by the pH of the soil in which they grow. It can either be sandy or chalky, as either would provide the vital drainage. If, however, yuccas were to be grown on a heavy clay soil, then it would be essential that a raised bed be provided, to give good drainage. They all will thrive in poor soils; this reflects the habitat to which they are adapted.

The other requirement for successful flowering is, in most cases, a good open sunny site. One exception to this is *Yucca × floribunda,* which will tolerate some shade and still flower well. *Yucca schotti* will also cope with some shade, but is not so hardy and will need shelter from cold winds.

The hardy species are also well able to live near the sea, particularly *Yucca recurvifolia* and *Yucca gloriosa*, which originate from a marine-edge environment.

In general, yuccas require little attention, although the old leaves that crowd around the trunk of some species can be removed. These should be carefully torn off, starting at the bottom and working up. A stout pair of gardening gloves is recommended, as the edges of the leaves can cut as well as any knife and safety glasses may be advised against the leaves' terminal spine. The old flower stalks are best left until the wind snaps them, as by then the plant will have grown to protect the point of attachment. If they are cut shortly after flowering, the open end is exposed to bacterial rots that are carried in rain into the yucca's open fibrous wood.

Tender Species

Tender species can be grown in John Innes No. 2, but extra sharp sand in the mix can be helpful; also, a collection of crocks and gravel in the bottom of the pot will assist the drainage. Recently I have been using the more environmentally friendly peat free compost, made from composted timber residues. To this base I add about one third sand and some blood, fish and bone. The results have been very good so far; the lighter texture of the compost seems to suit the yuccas.

A good sunny position is recommended, although *Yucca elephantipes* in particular will tolerate light shade. *Yucca elephantipes* naturally will form a large shrub or small tree, so it will eventually outgrow its position even when restricted in a relatively small pot. The cure is simple; during a warmer part of the year, cut it back with a saw to the required height, seal the cut end with a product like 'Arbrex', and wait for it to produce new shoots. Do not forget to pot up the off-cuts. During the growing season it is advisable to feed potted yuccas with a well-balanced fertilizer. They should be watered well, but then allowed to become fairly dry in between watering.

Propagation

To propagate yuccas, the easiest way is to break off small pieces of the underground stems [toes] of about 4-5 cm, these can then be potted up, or even planted directly into the ground; this is best carried out in late Spring or early Summer. The trunk-forming species can be propagated by the use of the end of a branch. A section of 5-20 cm can be cut off and placed in a compost mix containing a generous amount of sharp sand in pots and left to root.

The more unusual species may need to be produced from seed, available from specialist seed suppliers (See appendix III). Seeds should be placed in pots, which contain a gritty mix, in which the soil can be kept moist but not stagnant. As they germinate, then the level of watering should be reduced. A minimum temperature of 20° C is also required for a good result. I always sow the seed in June and then pot on when the seedlings start into growth in the following year.

Pests and Diseases

In general yuccas are trouble-free, although outdoor plants can suffer from attack by slugs and snails; these can be quite destructive to both the leaves and flowers. Snails in particular can harbour deep in the foliage; these may be removed by hand in soft leaved forms, otherwise slug pellets can be used.

The indoor specimens do seem susceptible to scale insects, which may position themselves along the leaves, where they can at least be washed off; but they may also lurk amongst the base of the leaves, where they are much more difficult to remove, but a good spray with a natural insecticide containing fatty acids should solve the problem.

Bacterial rots seem to be the other problem. These may enter as previously described after flowering, or they can occur from the roots up, particularly if there has been some over-watering.

Catalogue

The genus *Yucca* has been split into four subgenera, two of which were once regarded as genera in their own right. These sections follow in the text; within each section the species are in an order so similar plants are close to each other, this makes for easier comparisons. An inclusive attitude has been taken towards what is a taxonomically difficult genus. Yuccas can be quite variable, and due to apparent hybridisation, they can grade from one species to another.

Key to subgenera

1a Capsule indehiscent   2
1b Capsule dehiscent, leaf blade thin, mainly narrow (although in *Y. rupicola* and *Y. harrimaniae gilbertiana* broad), plano-convex, flexible, (although in *Y. h. gilbertiana* and *Y. h. neomexicana* concavo-convex and rather rigid), capsule dry, soon becoming erect, seed smooth, thin, flat, with or without marginal wing   3
2a Leaf blade large, broad, mainly thick, concavo-convex, rigid, sword-like, or in *Yucca schottii* somewhat thin and flexible; fruit large and fleshy, eventually becoming pendent and drying, often with gummy covering; seed rough, more or less thickened, flat, without marginal wing   subgenus **Yucca** (Engelmann) Watson (Section *Yucca* Engelmann; Section *Sarcocarpa* McKelvey).
2b Leaf blade small, thin, narrow, plano-convex, rigid, tip concavo-convex; fruit dry and spongy, erect, spreading or variously directed; seed smooth, thin, without marginal wing   subgenus **Clistocarpa** (Engelmann) McKelvey (Section *Clistocarpa* Engelmann).
3a Stigma lobed, capsule commonly septicidal or occasionally septicidally and loculicidally dehiscent, leaf margin with filaments   subgenus **Chaenocarpa** (Engelmann) McKelvey (Section *Chaenocarpa* Engelmann).
3b Stigma capitate, capsule loculicidally dehiscent, leaf margin without filaments   subgenus **Hesperoyucca** (Engelmann) Baker (Section *Hesperoyucca* Engelmann; *Hesperoyucca* (Engelmann) Clary – as genus).

Subgenus **Yucca** Watson
Key to Species

		go to
1a	Leaf margins filiferous	2
1b	Leaf margins not filiferous	3
2a	Inflorescence not pendent	4
2b	Inflorescence pendent	5
4a	Flowers 4 cm or more long	6
4b	Flowers less than 4 cm long	7
6a	Stemless or up to 1.5 m high	8
6b	Simple or many trunks, over 2 m	9
8a	Inflorescence less than 1 m high	1. *baccata*
8b	Inflorescence more than 1 m high	2. *thornberi*
9a	Perianth not fused	10
9b	Perianth fused	11
10a	6 or more branches	3. *arizonica*
10b	5 or fewer branches	12
12a	Leaves tapering from base to apex	4. *torreyi*
12b	Leaves widest near middle	13
13a	Flowers small 4-6 cm, globose	5. *schidigera*
13b	Flowers large 6-9 cm long, open	6. *grandiflora*
11a	Inflorescence 1.5-2 m high	7. *carnerosana*
11b	Inflorescence 1.3 m high	8. *faxoniana*
7a	Stemless	9. *endlichiana*
7b	One or more trunks	14
14a	Five or fewer branches	15
14b	Six or more branches	16
15a	Leaves thin, flexible, few fibres	10. *schottii*
15b	Leaves rigid	17
17a	Leaves concavo-convex, few fibres	11. *treculeana*
17b	Leaves linear-lanceolate	12. *mixtecana*

Key to Species

		go to
16a Leaves less than 35 cm long	**13. *valida***	
16b Leaves more than 35 cm long		18
18a Flowers less than 2 cm long	**14. *decipiens***	
18b Flowers more than 2 cm long		19
19a Leaves 2-3.5 cm wide	**15. *periculosa***	
19b Leaves 6-7.5 cm wide	**16. *jaliscensis***	
5a Fruit 15-20 cm long	**17. *declinata***	
5b Fruit 4-10 cm long		20
20a Branches many, leaf margins with white fibres	**18. *filifera***	
20b Branches few, leaf margins with grey fibres	**19. *potosina***	
3a Leaves less than 40 cm long, never flowers	**20. *desmetiana***	
3b Leaves more than 40 cm long, produces flowers		21
21a Leaves thick and flat	**21. *aloifolia***	
21b Leaves not thick and flat		22
22a Leaves narrow 5 mm or less	**22. *linearifolia***	
22b Leaves 5 mm or more wide		23
23a Produce several stems		24
23b Produce single trunk		25
24a Inflorescence more than 1 m		26
24b Inflorescence less than 1 m		27
26a Leaves 40-70 cm long rigid	**23. *gloriosa***	
26b Leaves 70 cm long, thin, flexible		28
28a Leaves 75 cm long, nearly flat, outer ones recurving	**24. *flexilis***	
28b Leaves 90-100 cm long, undulate	**25. *recurvifolia***	
27a Trunks do not expand at base, few branches	**26. *capensis***	
27b Trunks expand at base, multi-branched	**27. *elephantipes***	
25a Not epiphytic	**28. *madrensis***	
25b Epiphytic	**29. *lacandonica***	

Yucca baccata Torrey

1a *Y. baccata*, near Peridot, Arizona
1b *Y. baccata* subsp. *vespertina*, Salt River Canyon, Arizona
2 *Y. thornberi*

Vernacular Names: Blue Yucca, Banana Yucca, Datil, Fleshy Fruit Yucca.

Habit: Plants either simple or clumped at ground level, rhizomatous, may produce procumbent stems of 1.5 m, clump may contain up to 70 rosettes.
Leaves: 30-70 x 3.5-5 cm, widest towards the middle, usually straight, maybe incurved or twisted, deeply concave-convex, quite rigid, rough, margins usually have coarse short curly fibres, dead leaves reflex and cover stem.
Inflorescence: 35-80 cm high, in the form of a roughly ellipsoidal panicle, which forms within the leaves.
Flowers: Variable in size on different plants, 40-100 mm long, campanulate, a little pendent, white commonly tinged purple.
Style: 5-7 x 3.2 mm.
Fruit: Large, 17 x 5-6.5 cm, tapering from base to apex, weighing up to 500 grams.
Seeds: 7-11 mm, flat, thick, rough, dull black, wingless.
Flowering: April-June.
I have found this yucca to be hardy enough – but our wet climate seems to be the problem.

Key to Subspecies
1a. Forms loose groups, inflorescence 60-80 cm high   subsp. ***baccata***
1b. Forms dense groups, leaves blue-green, inflorescence 30-60 cm high   subsp. ***vespertina***

Subsp. *baccata* Torrey
Habit: Plants simple, stemless or form open clumps with two to six short procumbent stems.
Leaves: 30-70 cm long, dark green.
Inflorescence: 60-80 cm high.
Distribution: USA (southeast California, southern Nevada, southern Utah, southwest Colorado, Arizona, New Mexico, west Texas), Mexico (northern Chihuahua).
Habitat: Rocky hills, mountain slopes, grassy plains and woodlands of juniper and oak.
Altitude: 1000-2500 m.

Subsp. *vespertina* (McKelvey) Hochstätter

Synonyms: *Y. baccata* var. *vespertina* McKelvey; *Y. vespertina* (McKelvey) Welsh.
Habit: Plants stemless or with short procumbent stems, more erect than type, form dense confused clumps.
Leaves: 50-150 cm long, blue-green.
Inflorescence: 30-60 cm high.
Distribution: USA (northwest Arizona, south-eastern California, southern Nevada, extreme southwest Utah).
Altitude: 600-1700 m.

Yucca thornberi McKelvey

Synonyms: *Y. confinis* McKelvey; *Y. baccata* subsp. *thornberi* (McKelvey) Hochstätter.
Habit: Form crowded clump, 2-5.5 m wide, with 6-24 rosettes of leaves, stems 65-150 cm.

Leaves: 30-100 or even 130 x 1.2-4 cm, tapering from base to apex, or slightly broader near middle, straight or curved outward, mostly concavo-convex, usually smooth on both surfaces, yellow-green at maturity, more glaucous when young, margins have a few coarse fibres, terminal point stout and sharp, dead leaves reflex to cover stems.
Inflorescence: 1-1.3 m high, panicle protrudes from leaves by a quarter to half its length, on scape of 25-50 cm.
Flowers: Large, 75-125 mm, campanulate, white to cream.
Style: 5-7 x 3.2-5 mm.
Fruit: Large, 120-180 x 32-45 mm, tapering from base to apex.
Flowering: April-May.
Distribution: USA (southeast Arizona, southwest New Mexico), Mexico (northeast Sonora, northwest Chihuahua).
Altitudes: 1000-1600 m.

This plant seems to be regarded as a natural hybrid, possibly between *Y. baccata* and *Y. arizonica*, although Hochstätter in 2002 split this species into *Y. baccata* subsp. *thornberi* and *Y. confinis*. Here I have placed them together as suggested by Webber, who felt there was no real difference between them.

3 *Yucca arizonica* McKelvey

Habit: Tall ragged clump, 5 to 40 rosettes, trunks of 1-4.5 m.
Leaves: 30-65 x 1.4-3 cm, broadest toward middle, straight or somewhat incurved, predominantly concavo-convex, smooth, green, tinged yellow or blue, leaf margins have fine fibres, terminal spine present.
Inflorescence: 1-1.5 m, the upper two thirds forming an elongated panicle.
Flowers: 65-130 mm long, globose to campanulate.
Style: 5-7 mm and nearly as wide.
Fruit: 90-150 x 25-40 mm, slender, cylindrical, pendent.
Seeds: 5-10 mm long and wide, 2 mm thick, flat, dull black, wingless.
Flowering: April-May.
Distribution: USA (southern Arizona), Mexico (northern Sonora).
Habitat: Gravelly and rocky hills, mountain slopes and plateaus of desert grassland and woodland.
Altitude: 350-1350 m.

4 *Yucca torreyi* Shafer

Synonyms: *Y. baccata* var. *macrocarpa* Torrey; *Y. macrocarpa* (Torrey) Merriam; *Y. torreyi* forma *parviflora* McKelvey.
Vernacular Names: Palma.
Habit: 2.5-4.5 m high trunk, normally without branches.
Leaves: 30-100 x 3-5 cm, tapering from enlarged base to apex, moderately concavo-convex, rarely flattened, thick, rigid, rough on both surfaces, yellowish-green, margins with thick fibres.
Inflorescence: Ellipsoidal panicle on short scape, usually half in the foliage.
Flowers: Large, 65-80 mm and up to 100 mm long, almost globose or campanulate, cream tinged purple.
Style: 5-8 mm.
Fruit: 70-105 x 25-38 mm, cylindrical to ovoid.
Seeds: 5-8 x 6-9 mm, flat, thick, rough, dull black.
Flowering: March-May.
Distribution: USA (southern New Mexico, southern Texas), Mexico

3 *Y. arizonica*, Tombstone, Arizona
4 *Y. torreyi*, Phoenix Botanic Garden, Arizona
5 *Y. schidigera*, Chloride, Arizona
6 *Y. grandiflora*

(eastern Chihuahua, most of Coahuila, northern Nuevo Leon, and just into the neighbouring Durango and Tamaulipas).
Habitat: Grassy chaparral.
Altitude: 450-1500 m.

Yucca schidigera Roezl

Synonyms: *Y. mohavensis* Sargent; *Y. macrocarpa* Coville.
Vernacular Name: Mohave Yucca.
Habit: Produces normally 1-3 trunks, occasionally as many as 4-7, up to 2.5 m, sometimes with a few upright branches.
Leaves: 33-105 x 2.5-5 cm, broadest near the middle, deeply concavo-convex along most of length, thick, rigid, yellow-green, margins with thick coarse curly fibres.

Inflorescence: 50-125 cm, ellipsoidal, densely branched panicle, short scape.
Flowers: 40-65 mm long, globose, creamy-white, tinged lavender or purple.
Style: 1-2 mm.
Fruit: Variable, 90-110 x 30-38 mm, cylindrical, often with some constriction.
Seeds: 6-9 x 8-11 mm, flat, thick, rough, dull black.
Flowering: April-June.
Distribution: USA (southern California, extreme edge of northwest Arizona and southern tip of Nevada).
Habitat: Gravelly mountain and valley slopes in desert and chaparral.
Altitude: 300-2000 m.

Yucca grandiflora Gentry

Vernacular Name: Palma, Sahuiliqui.

Habit: Trunks 4-6 m, produce a few branches from the base.
Leaves: 70-100, occasionally 140 x 4-5 cm, narrow close to base, widest near middle, dark green, shiny, persistent down trunk, margins coffee brown, develop filaments with age, terminating in sharp coffee brown spine.
Inflorescence: 70-100 cm, in form of irregular open panicle, which can be erect or curved, on a short scape.
Flowers: 60-90 mm, open, on short pedicel.

Style: Forms a short beak.
Fruit: 20 x 5 cm with a curved terminal beak.
Seeds: Thick and round.
Flowering: February-April.
Distribution: Mexico (eastern Sonora).
Habitat: Hillsides of volcanic rock and limestone, in mixtures of wood and pasture.
Altitude: 600-1300 m.

7 *Yucca carnerosana* (Trelease) McKelvey

Synonym: *Samuela carnerosana* Trelease.
Vernacular Names: Palm Samandoca, Spanish Dagger, Palma Loca, Palm Barreta.
Habit: Produce a trunk of 2.5-5 m, occasionally more, usually one stem with one rosette, but may branch once or twice at 1.5-2 m above ground level.
Leaves: 55-115 x 5-7.5 cm, rigid, narrow at union with base, then widest near the centre before reducing down to the terminal spine, white marginal threads, dead reflexed leaves may cover the trunk.

7

Inflorescence: 1.5-2 m, the top half occupied by a nearly spherical panicle with a rather open structure.
Flowers: 65-95 mm long, perianth tube 18-30 mm long, white.
Style: 7 x 3 mm.
Fruit: 100 x 40 mm, widest toward the middle.
Seeds: 7-9 x 8-10 mm, stout, flat or hemispherical, rough.
Flowering: March-May.
Distribution: USA (Texas, confined to Brewster County), Mexico (eastern Chihuahua, northern Coahuila, also in a separate area of southern Coahuila, southwest Nuevo Leon, northeast Zacatecas and northern San Luis Potosi).
Habitat: Grows on rocky and bushy slopes.
Altitude: 1000-2200 m.

There is a view that *Y. carnerosana* may be considered a synonym of *Y. faxoniana* due to its close similarities, (M. and G. Irish (2000)). However I think the differences are sufficient to keep them as separate species.
I have found that this plant will do quite well in a pot, and recently it has also survived outside in a sheltered position.

7 *Y. carnerosana*
8 *Y. faxoniana*,
Boyce Thomson Arboretum, Arizona

8   *Yucca faxoniana* (Trelease) Sargent

Synonyms: *Y. australis* Trelease; *Samuela faxoniana* Trelease.
Vernacular Names: Palma, Palma de San Pedro.
Habit: Trunk to 4 m, but only rarely branching.
Leaves: 51-100 x 5.2-7.5 cm, rigid, strap-like, with white marginal threads.
Inflorescence: 1-1.3 m, broad panicle, rather openly branched, held mostly above leaves on a short stout scape.
Flowers: 57.5-82.5 mm long, perianth tube less than 15 mm long, white.

8

Style: 5-7 mm.
Fruit: 30-90 x 25-30 mm, slightly tapered above and below middle, constricted below tip to form slender curved beak.
Seeds: 5-8 x 7-10 mm, thick, flat or occasionally hemispherical, surface rough, dull black, wingless.
Flowering: March-April.
Distribution: USA (Texas, along the Rio Grande, Big Bend section), Mexico (central eastern Chihuahua and northern Coahuila).
Habitat: Rocky and gravelly mountain slopes.
Altitude: 1300-1600 m.

Another yucca that will do well in a pot, but also seems tough enough to try outside in a sheltered position.

9   *Yucca endlichiana* Trelease

Vernacular Name: Pitilla.
Habit: Stemless, with rhizomes.
Leaves: 50 x 1.5 cm, few, erect, thick, half round near base, narrowly 'V' shaped above, smooth, bluish-green, somewhat dappled beneath, margins brown sparingly filiferous, fibres stiff, recurving, becoming short and very thick near base, terminating in a very short thick grey point, basal part of leaf blackish-purple.
Inflorescence: Panicle, shorter than leaves, with many branches.
Flowers: Small, 25 mm long, creamy to dull purplish-brown.
Fruit: 20 x 25-30 mm, pendent, subglobose or broadly ellipsoidal, with thin flesh that dries quickly.
Seeds: 5-6 x 6-7 mm, thin.
Flowering: Mainly May.

Distribution: Mexico (Coahuila, Sierra de Parras, Sierra del Rosario and Sierra de Paila).
Habitat: Soils with rocky substrata.
Altitude: 1200 m.

Yucca schottii Engelmann

Vernacular Names: Hoary Yucca, Mountain Yucca, Sword Cactus, Amole.
Habit: Trunks rarely over 3-4 m, simple or with a few branches.
Leaves: 40-90 x 2.5-5.5 cm, smooth, divergently spreading, thin, flexible, blue-green, margin, thin occasionally with a few thin fibres, terminal spine small and blunt.
Inflorescence: 30-80 cm, narrow ellipsoidal, rather densely branched panicle, on very short scape.
Flowers: Small 20-35 mm, almost globose, white.
Style: 3 mm.
Fruit: 60-125 x 25-38 mm, round at base tapering at apex.
Seeds: 5-8 x 7-10 mm, thick and flat or rarely hemispherical, dull black and rough.
Flowering: July-August in the United States and April-August in Mexico.
Distribution: USA (southwest New Mexico, southeast Arizona), Mexico (northeast Sonora, northwest Chihuahua with another small pocket in western central Chihuahua).
Habitat: Grows in oak woods and shady canyon slopes.
Altitude: 1000-2100 m.

This plant has been re-examined by Lenz and Hanson (2000) who consider it is a hybrid between *Y. baccata, Y. elata* and *Y. madrensis*. This is one of the more unusual yuccas, worth growing for the blue-green leaves, providing all year round interest. It will flourish in a pot, but has also grown well in a sheltered position outside. This species is also unusual in being tolerant of some shade.

10 *Y. schottii*, Chiricahua National Monument, Arizona
11 *Y. treculeana*, Arizona Sonora Desert Museum, Tucson, Arizona

Yucca treculeana Carriere

Synonym: *Y. canaliculata* Hooker
Vernacular Names: Palma Pita, Coyol
Habit: Forms a group of trunks with variable heights, 2.5-5.5 m, the bark has irregular fissures, deep on old specimens.

11

Leaves: 50-100 x 2.5-5 cm, thick, rigid, concavo-convex, plano-convex near base, blue or yellow-green, terminating in a short, sharp, spine.
Inflorescence: 75-130 cm overall, scape short, 30 cm, ellipsoidal panicle normally half or more in the foliage.
Flowers: Small 20-40 mm, globose, greenish-cream to cream.
Style: 3.2-5 mm.
Fruit: 65-100 x 17-24 mm, cylindrical with abruptly tapering apex.
Seeds: 4-5 x 5-6 mm, flat, thick, rough, dull black, wingless.
Flowering: March-April.
Distribution: USA (southern Texas), Mexico (most of Coahuila also just touching into surrounding states).
Habitat: Flat areas of chaparral.
Altitude: 100-1600 m.

Yucca mixtecana García-Mendoza

Habit: Trunks 2.5-5 m, simple or with few branches, rhizomes may produce clumps of 10-25 stems.
Leaves: 40-65 (75) x 1.5-3 cm, linear-lanceolate or linear, erect, glaucous to greenish-yellow, margins with dark border, filiferous, threads fine and soft, terminal spine 5-10 cm, dark brown, canaliculated.
Inflorescence: 50-80 cm, panicle, on scape 20-30 cm, pubescent.
Flowers: Small 20-25 mm long, campanulate, pendent, whitish-yellowish.
Fruit: 50-80 x 20-25 mm, cylindrical, pendent.
Seeds: Drop-shaped, black.
Distribution: Mexico (south Puebla, northwest Oaxaca)
Habitat: Desert scrub.
Altitude: 1370-2200 m.

13 *Yucca valida* Brandegee

Vernacular Name: Palma
Habit: Produces a trunk of 3-12 m, grows in clumps, may branch from base or higher.

13

13 *Y. valida*
14 *Y. decipiens*, Boyce Thompson Arboretum, Arizona
15 *Y. periculosa*, Boyce Thompson Arboretum, Arizona
16 *Y. jaliscensis*

Leaves: 15-35 x 1.5-3 cm, lanceolate, densely distributed along stem, thin smooth, yellow-green, margins with grey curly fibres, terminal spine sharp.
Inflorescence: Short 30 cm, panicle pyramidal, somewhat pubescent, remaining half to three quarters submerged in foliage on short scape.
Flowers: 25-50 mm, campanulate, creamy-white, fragrant, produced on pedicels nearly as long as flowers.
Fruit: 25-45 mm, oblong, nearly black.
Seeds: 7 x 1.5 mm, with rough edges.
Flowering: March-April.
Distribution: Mexico (throughout the centre of Baja California).
Habitat: Grows on flat sandy soil or smooth slopes with gravel soils, in brushwood desert.
Altitude: 200-800 m.
Flowering: April-July.

This is another good pot plant; with its short leaves it is easy to accommodate.

14 *Yucca decipiens* Trelease

Vernacular Names: Palma China, Izote.
Habit: Forms trees up to 25 m, very rough barked, up to 90 branches.

14

Leaves: 58 x 2.5 cm, rigid, elongated, oblong-lanceolate, smooth, margins with coarse fibres, usually ending in a terminal spine.
Inflorescence: 1.5 m, panicle broadly ovoid on short scape, mostly glabrous.
Flowers: 9-15 mm long, cream white.
Fruit: 6-8 x 2 cm, oblong, pendent.
Seeds: 6-7 x 7-8 mm, thick.
Flowering: January-March.
Distribution: Mexico (central table land from southeast Durango, Zacatecas and west, San Louis Potosi).
Habitat: Well-drained flat ground with deep soils.
Altitude: 1800-2480 m.

This one does very well as a pot plant, and forms a neat rosette.

15 *Yucca periculosa* Baker

Vernacular Name: Izote
Habit: Trunk up to 15 m, with a smooth bark, old plants have many ascending branches.
Leaves: 35-50 x 2-3.5 cm, smooth, oblong to linear-lanceolate, margins with many fine brown curly filaments particularly on young plants, apex has a rather short point.

15

Inflorescence: 1 m panicle, broadly ovoid, compact, on a short scape.
Flowers: Small 35 mm long, creamy-white, on pedicels of 10-15 mm.
Style: Short.
Fruit: 50-80 x 25-32 mm, oblong pendent.
Flowering: March-April in the more inland part of its range but nearer the coast flowers July-August.
Distribution: Mexico (central Oaxaca, northern Oaxaca through Puebla, Tlaxcala and into adjacent Veracruz in two separate areas)
Habitat: Plains and valleys with deep soils, also hillsides with smooth slopes and shallow soils in the scrub desert.
Altitude: 1300-1650 m.

16 *Yucca jaliscensis* (Trelease) Standley

Synonym: *Y. schottii* var. *jaliscensis* Trelease.
Vernacular Names: Izote.
Habit: A tree up to 12 m, very branched, branches upright and thin.

16

Leaves: 40-100 x 6-7.5 cm, smooth, rigid, divergent, concave, glaucous blue-green with a few marginal fibres.
Inflorescence: 50-100 cm, narrow ellipsoidal panicle on a short scape, compact.
Flowers: Small, 22-38 mm, subglobose.
Style: 3 mm.
Fruit: 60-120 x 25-38 mm, rounded at base, conical at apex.
Seeds: 5-7 x 7-10 mm, wrinkled.
Flowering: July-August.
Distribution: Mexico (two small pockets in southern Jalisco and northern Colima, also western Guanajuato).

17 *Yucca declinata* Laferrière

Vernacular Name: Datil.
Habit: Forms trunk of 3-6 m at maturity, branching at the crown and suckering at the base.
Leaves: 50-140 x 5-6 cm, widest at midpoint, straight, deflecting toward trunk, concavo-convex, yellowish-green, margins smooth but form a few threads with time.
Inflorescence: Forms panicle of 1-1.3 m, usually pendent, glabrous.
Flowers: Small 40-50 mm long, white.
Fruit: 15-20 cm, oblong tapering at base.
Seeds: 10-15 mm, flat, black, slightly ovoid.
Distribution: Mexico (north central Sonora).
Habitat: Open woodland, on soils of limestone and volcanic origin.
Altitude: 750-900 m.

18 *Yucca filifera* Chabaud

Synonyms: *Y. australis* (Engelmann) Trelease; *Y. baccata* subsp. *australis* Engelmann.
Vernacular Names: Palma China, Palma Corriente, Izote, Maji or Baji, Tambasi
Habit: Forms trees of 10 m or more, old plants may develop as many as 40 branches.
Leaves: 55 x 3.6 cm, linear to oblanceolate, constricted near base, rigid, generally rough on both surfaces, leaf margin with curly white fibres particularly on young leaves.

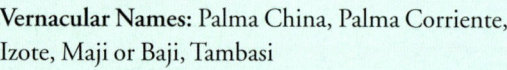

18

Inflorescence: Scape projects from leaves, panicle 1.5 m, pendular, more or less cylindrical, very floriferous.
Flowers: Small 38-52 mm, creamy-white, on pedicels of 27 mm.
Fruit: 50-88 x 27-33 mm, pendent, oblong, ending in a point.
Seeds: 8 x 2 mm, somewhat wrinkled.
Flowering: End of April to end of May.
Distribution: Mexico (southern Coahuila, then in a broad band through various states down as far as Mexico City).
Habitat: Flat ground with deep soils, in shrubby desert.
Altitude: 500-2400 m.

There are some really large specimens of this yucca in some of the Mediterranean gardens. I have found that it does well in a pot, over-wintered in a greenhouse. It has also been growing well, planted out in a sheltered position.

18 *Y. filifera*, Phoenix Botanic Garden, Arizona
19 *Y. potosina*
20 *Y. desmetiana*

Yucca potosina Rzesowski

Vernacular Names: Palma, Palma Barreta.
Habit: Tree of 2-7 m, with few branches.
Leaves: 30-100 x 3-6 cm, fat, rigid, somewhat concavo-convex, margins dark brown on inside and grey toward outside, with variable numbers of thin curled grey fibres, terminal spine grey.
Inflorescence: Pendular panicle, longer than leaves.
Flowers: Small, 25-50 mm, subglobose, white.
Style: Very short.
Fruit: 40-80 x 25-35 mm, oblong.
Seeds: 6-8 x 5-6 x 3-4 mm, obovoid.
Flowering: June-July.
Distribution: Mexico (central San Luis Potosi, in a small area).
Habitat: Hillsides with thin soils in brushwood and holm oak.
Altitude: 1700 m.

Yucca desmetiana Baker

Habit: Trunk forming, can attain heights of 2-3 m, but usually becomes recumbent.
Leaves: 40 x 2.5 cm, rigid, evenly and slightly recurved, green, tinged purple, margins smooth except slightly rough at the base, terminal spine not sharp.

The flowers and fruit of this plant are unknown, as is its precise origin, although it is believed to come from somewhere in northern Mexico. The similarity of the leaves to a very young *Yucca aloifolia* are quite striking and it may be that this plant is a *Yucca aloifolia* stuck in a juvenile form.
A plant that does well in a pot, but eventually sprawls about with its recumbent stems. Not hardy, but may hang on in a sheltered microclimate.

Yucca aloifolia Linnaeus

Synonyms: *Y. draconis* Elliot; *Y. crenulata* Haworth.
Vernacular Names: Spanish Bayonet, Spanish Dagger, Dagger Plant.
Habit: Slow growing shrubs or small trees, to 8 m, may form a simple erect stem, or be densely branched and often suckering at the base.
Leaves: 25-50 x 1.5-2.2 cm, thick, flat, rigid, margins denticulate, ending with brown, sharp terminal spine.
Inflorescence: Short, about 60 cm, panicle compact, usually close to the leaves.
Flowers: 60 mm long, pendular, globose, creamy sometimes tinged with purple.
Style: Short, not constricted, oblong and abruptly starting from the ovary.
Fruit: 100 x 50 mm, oblong, prismatic, nearly black, coreless, the seeds embedded in the dark purple pulp.
Seeds: 5-6 x 6-7 mm, glossy round or oval.
Flowering: October-December.
Distribution: USA (south eastern States), Central America and Caribbean. (Mostly due to cultivation).
Habitat: Found on flat ground or hills with gentle slopes on thin soils in tropical region.
Altitude: Up to 1800 m.

This plant is one of only two yuccas that are partly self-fertile. It will only tolerate slight frost, but will thrive in a pot, so is well worth growing. It does have teeth along the leaf margin and a sharp terminal spine to take into consideration, however.

Var. *yucatana* (Engelmann) Trelease
Synonym: *Y. yucatana* Engelmann.
Habit: Up to 8m high.

21a *Y. aloifolia* forma *marginata*
21b *Y. aloifolia* forma *tricolor*, La Mortola Gardens, Italy
21c *Y. aloifolia*
22 *Y. linearifolia*

Leaves: Rather flexible.
Inflorescence: Panicle flocculate.

▶ Forma *marginata* Bommer
Synonym: *Y. aloifolia* forma *variegata* Naudin.
Leaves: Green centre, borders margined with cream-white.

▶ Forma *tricolor* Bommer
Synonym: *Y. aloifolia* forma *medio-picta* Carriere.
Leaves: Green border and yellow to white central band, tinged red when young.

22 *Yucca linearifolia* Clary

Habit: Forms trunks 2-3.5 m, usually without branches.
Leaves: 34-38 x 0.4-0.5 cm, greyish-green, glaucous in new growth, linear, numerous, margins thin, pale yellow, minutely denticulate, terminal spine dark reddish brown to black, sharp, with age leaves reflex until they cover trunk.
Inflorescence: Panicle 60-80 cm on short scape, branches moderate in number, glabrous.
Flowers: Small, 30-33 mm, campanulate, creamy-white, pendent.
Style: 6-7 mm, tapering.
Fruit: 50-70 x 23-25 mm fleshy, asymmetrical, ovoid, with curved beak at apex.
Seeds: 5-7 x 4-6 mm, polymorphic, dull black.
Flowering: April.
Distribution: Mexico (south-central Nuevo Leon).
Habitat: Desert scrub vegetation, on shale.
Altitude: 1100-1300 m.

22

23 *Yucca gloriosa* Linnaeus

Vernacular Names: Adam's Needle, Spanish Dagger, Roman Candle, Palm Lily.
Habit: Develops a short trunk, 3-5 m, with several branches, caespitose.
Leaves: 40-70 x 5 cm, slightly glaucous when young, smooth or sometimes with roughened dorsal lines, thin, rigid, often concave particularly near the tip, margins usually brown with fine denticulation, may occasionally produce a few slender fibres, terminal spine sharp.

23a

Inflorescence: 60-150 cm high, mostly a narrow panicle, glabrous but occasionally slightly pubescent.

Flowers: Creamy-white, often tinged with red or violet.
Style: Oblong, white.
Fruit: Obovoid-oblong, mostly pendent with six ridges.
Seeds: 5-6 x 6-7 mm, glossy, slightly grooved.
Flowering: August-December.
Distribution: USA (South Carolina to northeast Florida).
Habitat: Coastal sand dunes.

This plant has been in cultivation since at least 1596 (Gerard, *Herbal*).

This plant makes a good architectural feature in the garden. There are two negative points: it has a sharp spine at the tip of the leaves; and it tends to flower late in the year, thus exposing the panicle to the risk of early frosts.

23c

23d

23b

▶ Forma ***marginata*** Carriere
Leaves: Bordered with pale green.

▶ Forma ***nobilis*** Carriere
Synonym: *Y. gloriosa* 'Ellacombei' Baker
Leaves: Occasionally with some folding, glaucous, outer ones recurved, sometimes twisted to one side.

▶ Forma ***variegata*** hort.
Leaves: Bordered with creamy-yellow stripe, fading to creamy-white on older leaves.

This form is well worth growing for its very striking leaves; these provide all year round interest. The two negative points that relate to the species also apply to this form.

23a Y. gloriosa
23b Y. gloriosa forma *marginata*
23c Y. gloriosa forma *nobilis*
23d Y. gloriosa forma *variegata*
25a Y. recurvifolia
25b Y. recurvifolia forma *variegata*
25c Y. recurvifolia forma *marginata*

24 *Yucca flexilis* Carriere

Habit: Develop a short trunk, branching to form clump of rosettes.
Leaves: 75 x 4 cm, mostly transiently glaucous, nearly plain, outer ones becoming recurved, margins finely denticulate or smooth, terminating in a spine.
Inflorescence: 1.2 m, loose panicle on a long scape.
Flowers: 90 mm long, white, pendent.
Style: Somewhat shouldered.
Fruit: Unknown.

A variable plant, which is only known in cultivation; it, however, closely resembles *Yucca recurvifolia*, but with narrower leaves.

25 *Yucca recurvifolia* Salisbury

Synonyms: *Y. recurva* Haworth, *Y. pendula* Groenland.
Habit: Produces woody stems up to 5m, but usually shorter, some branching.
Leaves: 90 x 6 cm, nearly flat or undulate, recurved, somewhat glaucous at first, margins yellow or brown, often with microscopic denticulation, or smooth and occasionally with a few filaments.
Inflorescence: 120 cm panicle, with broader branches than *Y. gloriosa*.
Flowers: 50-70 mm, creamy-white.
Style: Shouldered.
Fruit: Erect, oblong, with 6 winged ribs.
Seeds: 6-7 x 7-8 mm, dull black, surface grooved.
Flowering: July-September.
Distribution: USA (southern Alabama, southern Georgia northeast Florida, and on Dauphin, Ship and Breton Islands between mouths of the Mobile and Mississippi Rivers).

25a

25b

25c

This is the plant for any one who wants a good, reliable, large, hardy yucca. It should, once established, produce a large panicle every other year, and even more once mature.

Forma *marginata* (Carriere) Trelease
Leaves: Bordered with yellow and sometimes tinted rose.

Forma *variegata* (Carriere) Trelease
Leaves: Central yellow stripe.

26 *Yucca capensis* L. W. Lenz

Habit: Forms stem of 1-5.5 m, with time develops a rhizome and produces several stems that are usually without branches, older stems become recumbent, stems do not expand at ground level.
Leaves: 100 x 5 cm, linear-oblanceolate, constricted near the base, concavo-convex, moderately thin, flexible, margins dark grey, somewhat smooth to somewhat rough, without detaching fibres, tip sharp but without distinct terminal spine.
Inflorescence: 1 m, on a short scape, not exceeding the leaves, pubescent to glabrous, panicle broadly ellipsoidal.
Flowers: Variable to 100 mm long, cream-white.
Fruit: 115 mm long, oblong-cylindrical, pendent, fleshy, green drying to black.
Flowering: July-October, variable, as this depends on rain in summer.
Distribution: Mexico (Cape Region of Baja California).
Habitat: Subtropical deciduous forest and evergreen woodland.
Altitude: Sea level-1000 m.

27 *Yucca elephantipes* Regel

Synonym: *Y. guatemalensis* Baker.
Vernacular Names: Izote, Palmita, Itavo or Itabo, Kak-tuk, X-Tuk or Tuk

27a

Habit: Usually have several trunks, which become enlarged at the base, developing a rough bark with age, forms a compactly branched tree, 8-10 m high.
Leaves: 50-100 x 5-7.5 cm, rigidly spreading, clear green, glossy, plain or slightly folded, margins rough, also may be roughened on dorsal ridges, leaf tip soft.
Inflorescence: 60-100 cm, erect panicle that protrudes just beyond leaves, densely flowered.
Flowers: Small, 35 x 20 mm, white or creamy-white.

27b

27c

Style: Short, oblong.
Fruit: 70-80 x 45 mm, oblong-ovoid.
Seeds: 8-10 mm, more or less circular.
Flowering: February-July in subtropical regions.
Distribution: Mexico (In the wild along the coast of Veracruz).
Altitude: 1500 m.
Habitat: Hillsides in the tropical rainforest, where it is quite rare. This yucca, however, is extensively cultivated through Mexico and Central America.

This is the best known tender species, widely used for interior landscaping. It is well able to prosper even when very cramped in a pot and in part shade. There are some good variegated forms available, that add extra interest. The down side to this species, however, is that it will eventually make a large shrub or small tree, and so it is not usually practical to grow it to a size where it may flower.

▶ *Yucca elephantipes* 'Head Jewel'
Leaves: Bordered with pale green to creamy-white longitudinal stripe.

▶ *Yucca elephantipes* 'Jewel'
Leaves: Longitudinally striated cream and pale green throughout a large portion of centre.

▶ *Yucca elephantipes* 'Puck'
Leaves: Bordered with narrow longitudinal creamy white stripe.

▶ *Yucca elephantipes* 'Silver Star'
Leaves: Large central longitudinal band, striated pale green and silvery-white.

27a *Y. elephantipes*, a Mortola Gardens, Italy
27b *Y. elephantipes* 'Head Jewel'
27c *Y. elephantipes* 'Jewel'
27d *Y. elephantipes* 'Puck'
27e *Y. elephantipes* 'Silver Star'

27d

27e

28 *Yucca madrensis* Gentry

Vernacular Name: Soco.
Habit: Simple trunk up to 2 m.

Leaves: 50-100 x 2-3.5 cm, linear-lanceolate, thin, flexible, almost flat, glaucous blue-green to yellow-green, margins grey-brown, finely denticulate, terminal spine 5-12 mm, weak, fine, brown or grey.
Inflorescence: Panicle on a short scape, such that the flowers are half submerged amongst the leaves, branches short, pubescent.
Flowers: Small 35 mm long.
Fruit: 110-130 x 30-50 mm, rounded at base, generally asymmetrical.
Flowering: July.
Distribution: Mexico (eastern Sonora, western Chihuahua, in two small areas).
Habitat: Rough and sometimes rocky hillsides with pine and holm oak.
Altitude: 1350-2000 m.

29 *Yucca lacandonica* Gómez-Pompa and Valdés

Vernacular Names: Quim, Chis.
Habit: Epiphytic, producing horizontal curved stem, 2.5-3 m long which becomes enlarged toward base.
Leaves: 65 x 6 cm, constricted toward base, thin, both surfaces more or less smooth, margins yellowish and finely denticulate, sharp terminal spine.
Inflorescence: 40 cm, a small panicle on a short scape.
Flowers: 45 mm long, campanulate.
Fruit: 40 x 20 mm (immature), conical.
Seeds: 4.5 x 2.3 mm, thin even, no marginal wing.
Flowering: May, however, in the greenhouse flowered in September.
Distribution: Mexico (Two separate pockets, one in southwest Tabasco and northwest Chiapas, the other in eastern Chiapas and probably neighbouring Guatemala).
Habitat: It grows on trees up to 25 m up in the tropical rain forest.
Altitude: 300 m.

28 Y. madrensis
29 Y. lacandonica
30a Y brevifolia, south of Wikiup, Arizona
30b Y. brevifolia

Subgenus **Clistocarpa** Engelmann

Yucca brevifolia Engelmann

Synonyms: *Y. arborescens* (Torrey) Trelease; *Clistoyucca arborescens* (Torrey) Trelease.
Vernacular Names: Joshua Tree, Tree Yucca, Cactus Yucca, Yucca Palm.
Habit: Grows to form small trees of 6-9 m (though some specimens have been recorded at twice this size), trunk very stout at ground level, denuded of leaves, normally having only one stem but occasionally

30a

developing several, bark reddish brown or grey, rough, gashed with deep fissures that run horizontally and vertically, branches commencing at 0.6-1.3 m, or 2.5-3 m, above the ground, depending on subspecies, from then on continuing to fork every 0.6-1 m, the inner ones ascending, the outer ones horizontal or descending, the branches being clothed in a thatch of reflexed dead leaves near their ends.
Leaves: Cluster in a mature plant to cover up to the last meter of a branch, blade 15-40 x 0.6-1.6 cm, starts plano-convex, final third being concavo-convex, both surfaces smooth or slightly rough, inner surface has a slender median rib, glaucous pale blue or sage-green with a tough lemon yellow border containing straw coloured denticulation, terminates in a red-brown spine.
Inflorescence: 0.3-0.5 m, consisting predominantly of obovoid panicle.

Flowers: 40-70 mm, globose, each petal thick and fleshy, dull greenish-yellow to sage green or rarely cream.
Style: No larger than 1.6 x 1.6 mm.
Capsule: 65-100 x 45-65 mm, usually ovoid, tipped with remains of stigma and style, dry spongy interior.
Seeds: 8-11 x 9-12 mm, flat, slightly thickened, usually smooth.
Flowering: March-May.

The best known location is the 'Joshua Tree National Monument,' California.

30b

An essential plant for any yucca collector, but extremely demanding in our British conditions as it is not hardy and excessive rain soon rots the roots. Just to add to the difficulty, they like a deep root run, so do not last very long in pots, either. They are, therefore, yet another one to be planted directly into the ground within the greenhouse.

Key to Subspecies

1a. Rarely branched, dense groups of numerous trunks subsp. ***herbertii***
1b. Single or a few trunks 2
2a. 5-15 m tall, branching starts at 2-3 m high subsp. ***brevifolia***
2b. .3-6 m tall, branching starts at 0.5-1 m high subsp. ***jaegeriana***

Subsp. ***brevifolia*** Engelmann

Habit: Trunk 5-12 m, openly branched at 2-3 m above the ground.
Leaves: 15-40 x 0.6-1.6 cm.
Distribution: USA (southeast California, northwest Arizona, south Nevada and southwest Utah).
Habitat: High edges of the Mohave Desert, on desert plains and alluvial fans.
Altitude: 500-2000 m.

Subsp. ***jaegeriana*** (McKelvey) Hochstätter

Synonyms: *Y. brevifolia* var. *wolfei* Jones; *Y. brevifolia* var. *jaegeriana* McKelvey.
Habit: Trunk 3-6 m, densely branched at 0.5-1 m above ground.
Leaves: 10-20 x 1.5 cm.
Inflorescence: 30 cm long, with scape of 5 cm.
Flowering: April-May.
Distribution: USA (southern Nevada, just into adjacent California, Arizona and Utah).
Habitat: Mohave Desert and Great Basin Desert.
Altitude: 1000-2000 m.

Subsp. ***herbertii*** (Webber) Hochstätter.

Synonyms: *Y. brevifolia* forma *herbertii* Webber; *Y. brevifolia* var. *herbertii* (Webber) Munz.
Habit: 3-6 m, plants clumped with numerous trunks, rarely branched.
Leaves: 4-10 x 1.2 cm.
Flowering: April-May.
Distribution: USA (California, Los Angeles County, west end of Antelope Valley).

30c *Y. brevifolia* subsp. *jaegeriana*, Mesquite, Nevada
30d *Y. brevifolia* subsp. *herbertii*, Boyce Thompson Arboretum, Arizona

Subgenus **Chaenocarpa** Engelmann

Key to Species   go to

1a Leaf margin denticulate 2
1b Leaf margin filiferous 3

2a Plants with trunks 4
2b Plants without trunks 5

4a Leaves 3-5 mm wide   31. *queretaroensis*
4b Leaves wider than 5mm 6

6a Leaves 7-12 mm wide   32. *thompsoniana*
6b Leaves 12-17 mm wide 7

7a Leaves spreading rigidly .... 33. *rigida*
7b Leaves flexible .... 34. *rostrata*

5a Forms dense clumps, leaves 1-2 cm wide .... 35. *reverchoni*
5b Forms open clumps, leaves 2-4 cm wide 8

8a Mature leaves straight blue to grey-green .... 36. *pallida*
8b Mature leaves undulate and twisted, grey-green 9

9a Inflorescence branches recurved and drooping,   37. *cernua*
    capsule 32-45 mm long
9b Inflorescence branches erect ascending, capsule 48-75 mm 38. *rupicola*

3a Leaves flat and grass like 10
3b Leaves plano-convex or concavo-convex 11

10a Stoloniferous, clump forming 12
10b Not stoloniferous, form with time large open groups 13

12a Leaves rather abruptly tapering to tip, tip hooded, ... 39. *filamentosa*
    flowers 5-7 cm long
12b Leaves tapering, flowers 4-5 cm long .... 40. *flaccida*

13a Leaves 8-15 mm wide, capsule 30-45 mm long .... 41. *constricta*
13b Leaves 10-40 mm wide, capsule 40-70 mm long 14

14a Inflorescence a raceme or with a few branches, ... 42. *arkansana*
    flowers starting just above leaves, flowers whitish-cream
14b Inflorescence paniculate, flowers starting well above .... 43. *necopina*
    leaves, flowers greenish white

11a Inflorescence paniculate 15
11b Inflorescence racemose occasionally with a few branches 16

15a Inflorescence up to 1 m, flowers 10-12 cm long .... 44. *campestris*
15b Inflorescence over 1 m, flowers 4-6 cm long 17

17a Plants stemless, leaves concavo-convex, flowers ...... 45. *coahuilensis*
    4 cm long, capsule globose
17b Produce trunks but may be stemless, leaves plano-convex, 46. *elata*
    capsule oblong -cylindric flowers 45-57 mm long,

16a Leaves concavo-convex 18
16b Leaves plano-convex 19

18a Leaves 20 cm long, flowers 30-40 mm long .... 47. *nana*
18b Leaves 30-45 cm long, flowers 50-55 mm long .... 48. *harrimaniae*

19a Inflorescence 90-250 cm, flowers start above leaves .. 49. *angustissima*
19b Inflorescence 40-100 cm, flowers start amongst or 20
    just above leaves

20a Leaves 7-10 mm wide, style bright apple green, ... 50. *glauca*
    capsule 40-55 x 20 mm
20b Leaves 6 mm wide, style white, capsule 50-60 x 25 mm 51. *baileyi*

31   *Yucca queretaroensis* Piña Luján

31

Habit: Plants produce single trunks of 3-5 m, without branches, becoming covered by reflexed, persistent dead leaves, and in time developing into small rhizomatous colonies of 3-10 individuals of different sizes.
Leaves: Very numerous in rounded head, 40-50 x 0.3-0.5 cm, linear, rigid, straight, dull light green, plano-convex, margins yellow with fine teeth, dark brown terminal spine.
Inflorescence: Very branched panicle, oval, 60-80 cm, branches pubescent.
Flowers: Small 23-26 mm, campanulate to globose, creamy-white, pendent on pedicels of 15-20 mm.
Style: 6-8 mm, conical, pale green.
Capsule: 70 x 25 mm.
Seeds: 9 x 7 x 2 mm more or less triangular, even.
Flowering: April-June.
Distribution: Mexico (east Queretaro, west Hidalgo).
Habitat: Hills with rough slopes and alluvial fans.
Altitude: 1300m.

32   *Yucca thompsoniana* Trelease

Synonym: *Y. rupicola* var. *rigida* Engelmann.
Vernacular Names: Trans Pecos Yucca.
Habit: Normally have a simple trunk of 0.7-2.6 m, with a diameter of 12-15 cm, may fork once or twice occasionally, trunk entirely clothed in dead reflexed leaves, live leaves forming a neat asymmetrical terminal rosette.
Leaves: 18-30 x 0.7-1.2 cm, widest near centre, concave-convex to plano-keeled, rough on both surfaces, finely striate, a uniform pale yellow or blue green, leaf margin is minutely denticulate, yellow or brownish, with sharp terminal spine.
Inflorescence: 1-1.5 m, panicle forming the upper portion, densely flowered, with 20-30 branchlets.
Flowers: 35-67 x 12-35 mm, white, globose to campanulate.
Style: 4-6 mm, slender, slightly enlarged toward base, white.
Capsule: 32-57 x 13-20 mm, narrow ovoid, attenuating above to a slender fragile rather straight beak, capsules abundant, 50 plus not uncommon.

Seeds: 5-6 x 6-7 mm, flat, thin dull black.
Flowering: April-June.
Distribution: USA (Texas at southwest end of the Edwards Plateau) Mexico (Coahuila, from Trans Pecos area to Nuevo Leon, extreme western edge, Chihuahua extreme eastern tip).
Habitat: Growing on rocky slopes and hills.
Altitude: 300-400 m.

In habit this yucca is very similar to the closely related *Y. rostrata*, but not so attractive, and the teeth on the side of the leaves cut through skin like a knife.

Yucca rigida (Engelmann) Trelease

Synonym: *Y. rupicola* var. *rigida* Engelmann.
Vernacular Names: Palmita, Palmilla.
Habit: Form trunks of 3-5 m, usually without branches, sometimes with a few branches near top.
Leaves: 42-61 x 1.2-1.7 cm, thin, but spreading rigidly, becoming reflexed when dead and covering the trunk, glaucous, margins yellow and denticulate.

Inflorescence: 130-170 cm, ovoid panicle, densely floriferous, scape of 30-70 cm.
Flowers: 40-59 mm long.
Capsule: 35-70 x 18-25 mm, thick-walled, rough, oblong, tapering, with short out-curved points.
Seeds: 4-5 x 5-6 mm, dull black.
Flowering: March-April, creamy white.
Distribution: Mexico (western Coahuila, northeast Durango and a southeast corner of Chihuahua).
Habitat: Rough hillsides with shallow or stony soil.
Altitude: 1200-1500 m.

This plant, with its glaucous foliage and panicle of creamy white flowers, is spectacular when grown in optimum conditions. Unfortunately, it is not hardy and does not do well in a pot, therefore in the U.K. can only be grown planted out in a greenhouse.

Yucca rostrata Engelmann ex Trelease

Synonym: *Y. rostrata* forma *integra* Trelease.
Vernacular Names: Big Bend Yucca, Zoyate, Beaked Yucca.
Habit: Forms trunk up to 4.5 m, occasionally with a few branches, trunks covered in dead reflexed leaves.
Leaves: 25-60 x 1.2-1.7 cm, linear, broadest near the centre, flat to concavo-convex, flexible, glaucous, margins yellow and minutely denticulate, with terminal spine.
Inflorescence: Panicle 60-200 cm, somewhat pubescent, ellipsoidal to ovoid, up to 40 branchlets and densely covered in flowers, scape 30-100 cm.
Flowers: 42-47 mm, globose to campanulate, white.
Style: 6-14 mm. thin.
Capsule: 35-7 x 18-25 mm, symmetrical, yellow-brown, later dark brown to black, ending in a tough curved spine.
Seeds: 5 x 6-7 mm, thin, dull black, without marginal wing.
Flowering: March-May
Distribution: USA (Texas, Brewster County), Mexico (northern Chihuahua and Coahuila).
Habitat: Gentle slopes.
Altitude: 300-800 m.

This yucca is happy to live in a pot. In Germany and around the Mediterranean it also grows very well outside, therefore in the right microclimate in Britain it might be worth a try.

Yucca reverchoni Trelease

Synonyms: *Y. rupicola* Scheele, *Y. rupicola* Trelease.
Vernacular Names: San Angelo Yucca, Palma.
Habit: Stemless, normally solitary, but ultimately form a small dense clump with up to 25 rosettes.
Leaves: 25-55 x 1-2 cm, linear, widest near the centre, concavo-convex, quite rigid, straight, glaucous-green, margin yellow with fine teeth.
Inflorescence: Up to 1.5 m, long slender panicle held well above foliage, narrowly ovoid with a few branches.
Flowers: 38-6 mm, campanulate-globose, pendent, white or greenish-white.

Style: 9-20 mm, white to greenish.
Capsule: 38-59 x 19-31 mm, ellipsoidal, with a short beak.
Seeds: 5-6 x 6-7 mm, flat, thin, finely sculptured.
Flowering: May-June.
Distribution: USA (southern Texas), Mexico (northeast Coahuila).
Habitat: Rocky limestone ledges and gravelly plains.
Altitude: 400-1250 m.

Yucca pallida McKelvey

Vernacular Name: Pale Leaf Yucca.
Habit: Stemless, forms single rosette or open clump of 10-30 rosettes.
Leaves: 35 x 3.5 cm, blade flat and straight at maturity, glaucous blue-green, margins bright yellow with fine teeth, inrolled near terminal spine.
Inflorescence: Up to 2.5 m, scape of 0.6-1.3 m, panicle branched at base with racemose tip, flowers numerous, first opening along central stem then out along branches and up to racemose tip.
Flowers: Large 50-65 mm, campanulate, pendent, palest green with whiter margins.
Style: 13-20 mm oblong-cylindrical to slightly ovoid, white, occasionally a little twisted near the top.
Capsule: 45-50 x 13-20 mm, oblong-cylindrical, at first tan, later black, beak of about 10 mm.
Seeds: Small 4-6 x 2-3 mm, matt black with rough surface.
Flowering: April-June
Distribution: USA (north central Texas).
Habitat: Mainly Blackland Prairies.
Altitude: 200-300 m.

Yucca cernua Keith

Habit: Plants stemless, form solitary clumps with thick rhizomes.
Leaves: 40-70 x 3.5-6.5 cm, lanceolate, flat or concavo-convex, particularly concavo-convex just behind tip, older leaves becoming undulate and twisting, young leaves glaucous, becoming yellowish-green to olive green, margins yellow and denticulate, terminal spine sharp.
Inflorescence: 2-4 m, scape 1.5-3.2 m, panicle moderately to densely

floccose, branches up to 35 cm, characteristically recurved and drooping as they lengthen.
Flowers: 34-50 x 7.5-18 mm, campanulate, pendent, white or slightly greenish white.
Style: 8-17 mm.
Capsule: 32-45 x 20-25 mm, oblong-cylindrical, symmetrical, pendent.
Seeds: 5-7 x 4-6 x 0.5-1 mm, polymorphic, obovate to D shaped.
Distribution: USA (eastern Texas, Jasper and Newton counties).
Habitat: Open or slightly shaded areas, restricted to acidic clay soils.

38 *Yucca rupicola* Scheele

Synonym: *Y. rupicola* var. *tortifolia* Engelmann.
Vernacular Name: Twisted Leaf Yucca
Habit: Plants almost stemless and soon forming an open clump with up to 15 rosettes, each rosette spreading, but with few old leaves.
Leaves: 30-60 x 2-4 cm, very broad toward middle, obliquely twisted, light green with slight striation, flaccid, margins reddish brown, but occasionally yellow, minutely denticulate, terminates in a sharp spine.
Inflorescence: Slender scape 36-152 cm, panicle 24-48 cm, glabrous, narrow ovoid, branchlets 1-13 cm.
Flowers: 60-80 mm long, campanulate, pendent, white to greenish-white.
Style: 4-6 mm, tapering, white or greenish-white.
Capsule: 40-55 x 20-30 mm, ellipsoidal or somewhat cylindrical, tapering to a beak.
Seeds: 6-8 x 7-8 mm, flat, thin, dull black, with narrow marginal wing.
Flowering: April-June.
Distribution: USA (Texas on the Edwards Plateau).
Habitat: Limestone ledges and on grassy plains.
Altitude: 450-870 m.

39 *Yucca filamentosa* Linnaeus

Synonyms: *Y. concava* Haworth, *Y. smalliana* Fernald.
Vernacular Names: Silk-grass, Spoon Leaf Yucca.
Habit: Plants stem-less, caespitosely suckering, to form large clump.
Leaves: 30-80 x 3.5 cm, grass like, thick concave, rigid, rough on both surfaces, particularly when dry, oblong lanceolate, leaf tip blunt and hooded just below the spine, margins with numerous twisting threads.
Inflorescence: 1.5-3 m or possibly higher, freely branching panicle

38 *Y. rupicola*
39a *Y. filamentosa*
39b *Y. filamentosa* 'Bright Edge'

occupying slightly more than the upper half, normally branches glabrous.

Flowers: 50-70 mm long, whitish.
    Style: 10 mm long, slight restrictions at base.
    Capsule: Thick, cylindrical to short ovoid, often constricted near middle.
    Seeds: 6-7 x 3-5.5 mm, glossy, black.
    Flowering: June-September.

There are some very good garden forms of this species to be found in Britain and elsewhere in Europe. They produce quite spectacular panicles of flowers and there are also some striking variegated forms. This species has the added attraction that the terminal leaf spine is not sharp. Also, it does well in a good-sized pot, hence is suitable for use as a patio plant.

Key to Subspecies

1a. Leaves ligulate to spatulate, surface coarse   subsp. *concava*
1b. Leaves not ligulate to spatulate   2
2a. Leaves broad erect, straight, surface coarse   subsp. *filamentosa*
2b. Leaves narrow, erect, surface smooth   subsp. *smalliana*

Subsp. *filamentosa* Linnaeus

Habit: Short subterranean stem, laterally branched forming variable groups of rosettes.
Leaves: 20-60 x 2.5-3 cm, erect, stiff, linear-lanceolate, cuspidate, Bluish-green to green, margins with strong twisted fibres

Inflorescence: 2-3 m, panicle with short branches up to 15 cm long, glabrous.
Flowers: 50-70 mm, white with pale green mid stripes.
Capsules: 30-60 mm, cylindrical, brownish when ripe.
Seeds: 4-7 mm.
Flowering: June-July.
Distribution: USA (Florida-New Jersey).
Habitat: Sandy soil in grassland, rarely in forest margins.
Altitude: Sea level.

Subsp. *smalliana* (Fernald) Hochstätter

Synonym: *Y. smalliana* Fernald.
Habit: Acaulescent, forming small clumps of rosettes.
Leaves: 20-40 x 1.5-3 cm, linear to lanceolate, smooth, margin with twisted fibres.

Inflorescence: 1.5-3 m, panicle with long branches, held well above the leaves.
Flowers: 50-60 mm, campanulate, white.
Capsule: 20-30 mm, cylindrical, not constricted, brownish when ripe.
Seeds: 8 x 4 mm, matt black.
Flowering: May-June.
Distribution: USA (central to northern Florida, near coast, south Georgia).
Altitude: Sea level.

▶ Subsp. *concava* (Haworth) Hochstätter
Synonym: *Y. concava* Haworth.
Habit: Single or in small group of rosettes.
Leaves: 20-40 x 1.5-3.5 cm, stiff, erect, spatulate, rough, dark green with marginal fibres.
Inflorescence: 1-2.5 m, panicle with short or long branches, held well above the leaves.
Flowers: 50-60 mm, campanulate, white.
Capsules: 20-40 mm, cylindrical, constricted, green, pale green when ripe.
Seeds: 6 x 3 mm, matt black.
Flowering: April -May.
Distribution: USA (North and South Carolina).
Habitat: Sand dunes and grassland.

Cultivars

Yucca filamentosa 'Bright Edge'.
Leaves: Margins golden yellow.
This is a good variegated form that produces a good show all year round.

Yucca filamentosa 'Color Guard'.
Leaves: Broad, wide creamy yellow stripe down the centre. A Japanese patented clone.

Yucca filamentosa 'Eisbär'.
Inflorescence: 1.5 m, with a graceful panicle of white flowers.
Flowers: July-August.
A variety selected by the German horticulturist Karl Foerster. This plant will bloom even when young.

Yucca filamentosa 'Elegantissma'.
Inflorescence: 1-1.2 m, panicle of white flowers.
Another variety of Karl Foerster.
Yucca filamentosa 'Glockenriese'.
Flowers: Large, creamy-white.
This variety has been attributed to Karl Foester.
Yucca filamentosa 'Gilt Edge'.
Leaves: Variegated form, with quite narrow leaves and pale yellow borders.
This is another good strong variant, very similar to 'Bright Edge'.
Yucca filamentosa 'Rosenglocke'.
Leaves: Large, having a tendency to corrugate, margins with several long thin curly white fibres.
Inflorescence: 1.6 m, the top 1 m forming a narrow panicle.
Flowers: Large, pendent, creamy-white, tinted pink on the outside.
Yucca filamentosa 'Schellenbaum'.
Leaves: Blue-green with recurved tips.
Inflorescence: 1.8 m.
Flowers: Campanulate, milk-white, on reddish brown pedicels.
Flowering: July-August.
Another variety selected by Karl Foester.
Yucca filamentosa 'Schneefichte'
Inflorescence: 1.8 m.
Flowers: Campanulate, long, pointed, milk white.
This is another of Karl Foester's forms, later blooming in comparison with other varieties.

39f

39c *Y. filamentosa* 'Color Guard'
39d *Y. filamentosa* 'Glockenreise'
39e *Y. filamentosa* 'Gilt Edge'
39f *Y. filamentosa* 'Rosenglocke'
39g *Y. filamentosa* 'Schneetanne'
39h *Y. filamentosa* 'Schellenbaum'
39i *Y. filamentosa* 'Schneeficte'

39g 39h 39i

Yucca filamentosa 'Schneetanne'.
Habit: Produces asymmetrical rosette.
Leaves: Rigid, blue-green.
Inflorescence: 1.6 m, the top 1m forming a panicle.
Flowers: Broad campanulate, creamy-yellow.
Flowering: July-August.
Another variety of Karl Foester.
Forma ***variegata.***
Leaves: Borders creamy-white, leaf centre dark glaucous-green, may become pink tinged particularly when under physiological stress.
Flowers: White.
This form does not seem very vigorous, and is very difficult to keep growing for very long.

Yucca flaccida Haworth

Vernacular Name: Flaccid Leaf Yucca.
Habit: Stemless, caespitose, forming clumps.
Leaves: Green to glaucous-green, lanceolate, thin, flexible, outer ones almost always recurved, with time develop long, rather straight thin fibres.
Inflorescence: Panicle of 0.5-1 m, pubescent.
Flowers: 40-50 mm long, green in bud, opening greenish-white.
Style: No restriction at base.
Capsule: Dull greyish-green, variously and irregularly flattened as if shaved with a knife.
Seeds: 7-8 x 8-10 mm, dull black.
Flowering: July-August.
Distribution: USA (North Carolina to Alabama, especially on the Blue Ridge and Appalachian Mountains).
Habitat: Dry stony places.

A good garden plant. The panicle and flowers are slightly smaller than the closely related *Y. filamentosa*, but the terminal spine on the leaves is almost nonexistent.

Cultivars
Yucca flaccida 'Golden Sword'.
Leaves: Broad golden yellow stripe running longitudinally through the centre.
A very spectacular plant, the leaves alone brightening up the garden all year round. I have, however, never seen a specimen flower.

40a *Y. flaccida*
40b *Y. flaccida* 'Ivory'
40c *Y. flaccida* 'Golden Sword'
40d *Y. flaccida* striated cultivar
41 *Y. constricta*

Yucca flaccida 'Ivory'.
Flowers: Campanulate, creamy-white stained green, held horizontally on a short pedicels. The flowers are held open and not hanging down, which is more normal for this genus.
A free-flowering form raised by Rowland Jackman of Woking, Surrey.

Yucca flaccida **striated cultivar**
Leaves: Distinctive; at base have creamy-yellow central band, towards the tip breaking down into a mixture of cream and green streaks.
Inflorescence: 80 cm, pubescent.
Flowers: Creamy-white with hints of green and purple.
This plant would appear to be a sport of *Y. flaccida* 'Golden Sword'. The author's specimen has even shown signs of reversion. The flower size and structure suggest that this plant should be renamed *Y. filamentosa*.

41 *Yucca constricta* Buckley

Synonyms: *Y. tenuistyla* Trelease; *Y. louisianensis* Trelease.
Vernacular Name: Buckley Yucca.
Habit: Plants either stemless or with short procumbent stems up to 0.4m, forming an open clump with one to twenty rosettes.
Leaves: 20-50 x 0.8-1.5 cm, linear, nearly flat or plano-convex, pale to dark green with white margins that become filiferous.

Inflorescence: 2-3 m, ovoid panicle that will at best occupy the top 0.5 m.
Flowers: Small, 50 mm long, globose, pale greenish-white.
Style: 8-11 mm, cylindrical with basal lobes extending slightly over ovary, whitish-green or pale green.
Capsule: 30-45 x 15-20 mm, oblong-cylindrical, deeply constricted.
Seeds: 5 x 8 mm, glossy black, with broad marginal wing.

Flowering: April-June.
Distribution: USA (from south to central Texas).
Habitat: Brushwood and grassland.
Altitude: 300-800 m.

My specimens of this yucca have all grown to a good size outside; but took nine years to flower.

42 *Yucca arkansana* Trelease

Synonyms: *Y. angustifolia* var. *mollis* Engelmann; *Y. glauca mollis* Branner and Coville.
Vernacular Name: Arkansas Yucca.
Habit: Plants either stem-less or with short prostrate stem, producing either a single rosette or small open clump of asymmetric rosettes.

42a

Leaves: 20-60 x 0.7-2.5 cm, straight, flat, grass-like, blue-green or yellow-green, papery white margins separating to fine curly fibres.
Inflorescence: Raceme up to 1 m, with few branches, to panicle of up to 2.5 m, carrying about twenty flowers.
Flowers: 32-65 mm, globose, whitish-cream, tinged with green or red.
Style: 7-13 mm, darker than ovary, swollen toward base, ovoid.
Capsule: 4-7 cm, stout, oblong-cylindrical, often asymmetrically constricted near middle.
Seeds: 7-8 x 10 mm, dull black.
Flowering: April-July.
Distribution: USA (central to north-central Texas, Oklahoma, west Arkansas).
Habitat: Prairies, on limestone outcrops and rocky soils.

This species has been growing quite well in my garden, but took nine years to flower.

Key to Subspecies

1a. Inflorescence up to 1 m high, with few branches
                                          Subsp. ***arkansana***
1b. Inflorescence over 1 m high, with many branches   2

2a. Inflorescence 1-2.5 m high, flowers 3-6 cm long, capsule deeply constricted   Subsp. ***louisianensis***
2b. Inflorescence 1-1.8 m high, flowers 3-3.8 cm long, capsule somewhat constricted   Subsp. ***freemanii***

42a Y. arkansana
42b Y. arkansana subsp. *louisianensis*

▶ Subsp. *arkansana* Trelease
Leaves: 1-2 cm wide.
Inflorescence: Up to 1 m, raceme or with few branches.
Flowering: July.
Distribution: USA (south-central, north and east Texas, central and northeast Oklahoma, west-southwest Arkansas).
Habitat: Prairies.

▶ Subsp. *freemanii* (Shinners) Hochstätter
Synonym: *Y. freemanii* Shinners.
Vernacular Names: Freeman Yucca.
Leaves: 1- 4 cm wide.
Inflorescence: 1-1.8 m, panicle with many branches.
Flowering: June.
Distribution: USA (northeast Texas, southwest Arkansas, northwest Louisiana).
Habitat: Grassland in sandy soil.

▶ Subsp. *louisianensis* Hochstätter.

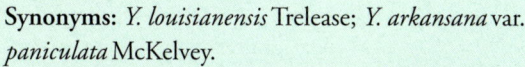
42b

Synonyms: *Y. louisianensis* Trelease; *Y. arkansana* var. *paniculata* McKelvey.
Vernacular Names: Grass Yucca, Louisiana Yucca.
Leaves: 2-3 cm wide.
Inflorescence: 1-2.5 m, forms panicle with many branches.
Flowering: May-June.
Distribution: USA (central and east Texas, south Arkansas, north and central Louisiana).
Habitat: Sandy soil among sparse pine and oak woods.

43 *Yucca necopina* Shinners

Habit: Stemless or with short prostrate stem, forming an open clump.
Leaves: 45-70 x 2 cm, flat and grass like, margins papery white with a few filaments.
Inflorescence: 1-3 m, either a raceme or panicle with ascending branches well above leaves.
Flowers: 30-60 mm long, greenish-white.
Capsule: 40-65 x 20 mm.
Flowering: April-June.
Distribution: USA (north and central Texas).

Shinners considered it a possibility that this plant may just be a hybrid between *Y. pallida* and *Y. arkansana*.

44 *Yucca campestris* McKelvey

Vernacular Names: Plains Yucca.
Habit: Form a dense clump with many rosettes, sometimes without, but may have a short stem, 0.6-1 m long.

44

Leaves: 65 cm, slender, wiry plano-convex, blue-green, margins at first white and finely filiferous becoming smooth.
Inflorescence: 0.6-1 m, panicle ellipsoidal, taking up more than the top half.
Flowers: 10-12 cm, globose, dull greenish-white, sometimes with a pinkish tinge.
Style: Green, darker than ovary, stout ovoid.
Capsule: 35-53 x 30-50 mm, rather stout with thin walls.
Seeds: 1.3 x 1 cm, shiny black.
Flowering: April-June.
Distribution: USA (endemic to western Texas).
Habitat: Plains, in deep sand dunes.

These are plants that struggle in our long wet winters. Mine, growing outside, show no intention of flowering. They are naturally found in deep sandy soils, so if these conditions can be provided they may well do better.

45 *Yucca coahuilensis* Matuda and Piña Luján

Habit: Plants stemless.
Leaves: Very numerous, 73-80 x 1-1.2 cm, concavo-convex, margin white or grey with filaments.

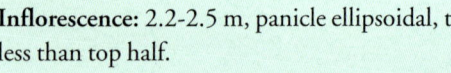

45

Inflorescence: 2.2-2.5 m, panicle ellipsoidal, taking up less than top half.
Flowers: 4 cm long, white.
Style: Short.
Capsule: 70 x 35 mm, globose.
Flowering: May-June.
Distribution: Mexico (southern Coahuila).
Habitat: Dry soils with natural pastures and desert scrub.
Altitude: Up to 360 m.

This plant is becoming increasingly rare, due to the growing amount of cattle ranching.

44 *Y. campestris*
45 *Y. coahuilensis*
46a *Y. elata*, Benson, Arizona

46 *Yucca elata* Engelmann

Synonyms: *Y. radiosa* Engelmann; *Y. angustifolia* Havard.
Vernacular Names: Soap Tree, Soapweed, Palmella.
Habit: Produce a trunk of up to 5m or more, simple or with a few branches.

46a

Leaves: 30-95 x 0.4-1.5 cm, linear, plano-convex, glaucous-green, margin white or bright green, developing fibres with age.
Inflorescence: 1.5-3.5 m, approximately the top half being occupied by the broad multi-branched, ellipsoidal panicle.
Flowers: 45-57 mm, campanulate-globose, pale yellow-green with whitish margins, occasionally pure white.
Style: Slender to stoutish, oblong-cylindrical or slightly obovoid, with well defined shoulders and short abruptly tapering stout neck.
Capsule: 50-82 x 25-40 mm, usually symmetrical, rarely constricted, oblong-cylindrical.
Seeds: 7-10 x 9-14 mm, thin, dull black, with or without marginal wing.

In my garden, the subspecies *Y. elata* subsp. *verdiensis* has always done well outside, although it did take ten years to flower. By contrast, the species type has failed to thrive outside, and I can only grow it planted directly into the ground within a greenhouse (it does not do well in a pot, as it requires a deep root run). However, in Germany, it seems to grow well outside and has flowered.

Key to Subspecies

1a. Inflorescence less than 2 m	subsp. ***utahensis***
1b. Inflorescence more than 2 m	2
2a. Produce trunk up to 5 m plus, leaves flexible	subsp. ***elata***
2b. Produce little or no trunk, leaves stiff	subsp. ***verdiensis***

Subsp. *elata* Engelmann

Habit: Form trunk up to 5 m or more, simple or with a few branches.
Leaves: Flexible.
Inflorescence: Up to 3 m.
Seeds: smooth.
Distribution: USA (south Arizona, south and central New Mexico west Texas), Mexico (northeast Sonora, northwest Chihuahua and central northern Coahuila).
Habitat: Desert and grassland.
Altitude: 500-2000 m.

▶ ### Subsp. *utahensis* (McKelvey) Hochstätter
Synonyms: *Y. utahensis* McKelvey; *Y. elata* var. *utahensis* (McKelvey) Reveal.

Vernacular Name: Utah Yucca.
Habit: May be with or without short stem.
Leaves: Flexible.
Inflorescence: Less than 2 m.
Seeds: Surface sculptured.
Distribution: USA (southwest Utah and north Arizona, into Grand Canyon Area).
Habitat: Sandy soil under creosote bushes and other vegetation.
Altitude: 850-2200 m.

▶ ### Subsp. *verdiensis* (McKelvey) Hochstätter
Synonyms: *Y. verdiensis* McKelvey, *Y. elata* var. *verdiensis* (McKelvey) Reveal

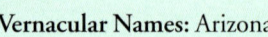

Vernacular Names: Arizona Yucca.
Habit: Stemless or with very short stem.
Leaves: Stiff.
Inflorescence: Up to 3 m.
Seeds: Sculptured.
Distribution: USA (Arizona, Yavapai Co., Gila Co., Navajo Co.).
Habitat: Sandy soil, with sagebrush.
Altitude: 900-2000 m.

47 *Yucca nana* Hochstätter

Vernacular Name: Dwarf Yucca.
Habit: Forms rhizomes, stemless, with single rosette or clump of rosettes.

Leaves: Up to 20 x less than 1 cm, concavo-convex, stiff erect, smooth, dark-green, filiferous along edge, with brownish terminal spine.
Inflorescence: Over 1 m raceme, with about 20 branchlets, 1-3 flowers per branchlet.
Flowers: Small 30-40 mm long, white, globose to ovoid.
Style: 10 mm long, cream.
Capsule: 3-4 x 2-3 cm, spherical to ovate, pendent, woody, green when ripe.

Seeds: 0.5-0.9 mm, flat, rough, hemispherical shape variable, black.
Flowering: April-June.
Distribution: USA (Utah, Great Basin Desert).
Habitat: Gravelly and sandy slopes in open pinewoods and sagebrush.
Altitude: 1600-2075 m.

48 *Yucca harrimaniae* Trelease

Synonym: *Y. colo-ma* Andrews.
Vernacular Name: Harriman Yucca
Habit: Plants either stemless or with short stem, form one rosette or a small clump of several rosettes.
Leaves: 30-45 x 0.7-4 cm, the widest point well above middle, usually straight, normally concavo-convex, at first pale sage green, eventually dark blue-green to yellow- green, smooth to rough on both surfaces, leaf margins at first papery, later developing long, straight, fine to coarse fibres, terminal spine short and sharp.
Inflorescence: 40-140 cm, racemose, about half forming a scape.
Flowers: Medium size, 50-55 mm long, rather globose, white,
Style: 10-14 x 3 mm, very slender, bright green.
Capsule: Small, 45-57 x 13 mm, slender, usually symmetrical, sometimes constricted, oblong-cylindrical, tipped with short curved beak.
Seeds: Small, rough, dull black with narrow marginal wing.
Flowering: April-July.
Altitude: 1000-2700 m.

This is another species where hardiness is not a problem, but our winter wet is. It also does not do well in pots for very long. A challenging plant to grow.

Key to Subspecies

1a. Inflorescence up to 40 cm, capsules absent, leaves scarcely filiferous   subsp. ***sterilis***
1b. Inflorescence 40-140 cm, capsules produced, leaves filiferous   2
2a. Inflorescence 1 m, flowers yellow to greenish   subsp. ***gilbertiana***
2b. Inflorescence 40-140 cm, flowers white   3
3a. Leaves 7-40 mm wide, flowers 4-6 cm long   subsp. ***harrimaniae***
3b. Leaves 7-20 mm wide, flowers 2-4 cm long   subsp. ***neomexicana***

48a

46b Y. elata subsp. *utahensis,* nr Kanab, Utah
46c Y. elata subsp. *verdiensis,* nr Cornville, Arizona
47 Y. nana
48a Y. harrimaniae, nr Grover, Utah

▶ Subsp. *harrimaniae* Trelease
Habit: Without rhizomes, rosettes in groups.
Leaves: 7-40 mm wide, rigid, erect, filiferous.
Inflorescence: 40-140 cm.
Flowers: 40-60 mm, white.
Distribution: USA (central southern and southeast Utah, southwest Colorado, northeast Arizona, north New Mexico).
Habitat: Grassland, sagebrush, pinyon-juniper, mountain brush, on desert ridges and hills.

▶ Subsp. *gilbertiana* (Trelease) Hochstätter

Synonyms: *Y. harrimaniae* var. *gilbertiana* Trelease, *Y. gilbertiana* (Trelease) Rydberg
Vernacular Name: Salt Lake Desert Yucca.
Habit: Forms rhizomes, rosettes in dense groups.
Leaves: Stiff, margins filiferous.
Inflorescence: Up to 1m.
Flowers: Yellow to greenish.
Seeds: 4-6 x 3-4 mm, roughly sculptured, black.
Distribution: USA (Utah, Creek Range, Snake Valley; Nevada, Goshut Indian, Pleasant Valley, Snake Range).
Habitat: Sagebrush vegetation and mountain slopes.

▶ Subsp. *neomexicana* (Wooton and Standley) Hochstätter

Synonyms: *Y. neomexicana* Wooton and Standley; *Y. harrimaniae* var. *neomexicana* (Wooton and Standley) Reveal.
Vernacular Name: New Mexico Yucca.
Habit: Forms rhizomes, rosettes widespread.
Leaves: 7-20 mm wide, stiff, filiferous.
Inflorescence: 40-140 cm.
Flowers: 20-40 mm long white sometimes tinged violet.
Distribution: USA (southwest Colorado, northeast New Mexico, northwest Oklahoma in the border area where it adjoins New Mexico).
Habitat: Semi-arid grassland.

▶ Subsp. *sterilis* (Neese and Welsh) Hochstätter
Synonym: *Y. harrimaniae* var. *sterilis* Neese and Welsh.
Vernacular Names: Sterile Uintah Basin Yucca.
Habit: Forms rhizomes, rosettes widespread.
Leaves: Recurved and flexible, leaning toward and on the ground, margins with few filaments.

Inflorescence: Up to 40 cm.
Capsule: None (asexually reproductive).
Distribution: USA (Utah, Duchesne Co. and Uintah Co.).

Yucca angustissima Engelmann.

Vernacular Name: Narrow Leaved Yucca.
Habit: Stemless or with a short procumbent stem, forms large clumps of twenty or more rosettes.
Leaves: 25-60 x 0.4-1.5 cm, striated, plano-convex, flexible, blue-green, margins white or greenish-white with a few loose curly fibres.
Inflorescence: 90-250 cm, usually in a raceme, occasionally with a few short branchlets, flowers start above the leaves.

Flowers: 45-57 mm, pendent, campanulate-globose, white to cream tinged purple on outside.
Ovary: 10-25 mm.
Style: 10-13 mm, slender, oblong-cylindrical, white or pale green.
Capsule: 35-50 x 20-23 mm, oblong-cylindrical, usually constricted near middle.
Seeds: 5-7 x 7-8 mm thin, dull black with narrow marginal wing.
Flowering: May-June.
Distribution: USA (north and central Arizona, parts of southern Utah and northwest New Mexico).
Habitat: Dry slopes of rock or sand, in grass and woodland.
Altitude: 800-2500 m.

This species is quite hardy outside, but does not seem to thrive. It appears that our long wet winters take their toll. Where a sandy soil can be provided then it may grow with more vigour. I have grown these plants for nearly ten years, but none have yet reached a size sufficient to flower.

Key to Subspecies

1a. Capsule large, 45-75 mm, somewhat constricted　　　　　2
1b. Capsule small, 35-55 mm, deeply constricted　　　　　　3
2a. Leaves 25-60 cm, long, flowers 30-45 mm long　　subsp. ***toftiae***
2b. Leaves 45-75 cm long, flowers 55-65 mm long　subsp. ***kanabensis***
3a. Leaves 25-45 cm long, flowers 45-55 mm long
　　　　　　　　　　　　　　　　　　　　　subsp. ***angustissima***
3b. Leaves 40-60 cm long, flowers 35-45 mm long　　　subsp. ***avia***

▶ **Subsp. *angustissima* Engelmann**
Leaves: 25-45 cm.
Inflorescence: 50-150 cm.
Flowers: 45-55 mm.
Style: 10-13 mm.
Capsule: Small, 35-50 mm, deeply constricted.
Distribution: USA (southwest Utah, north and central Arizona, northwest New Mexico).
Habitat: Flat desert or on mesas, mostly in sandy soil.
Altitude: 1000-2550 m.

▶ **Subsp. *avia* (Reveal) Hochstätter**
Synonym: *Y. angustissima* var. *avia* Reveal.
Vernacular Name: Avia Yucca.
Leaves: 40-60 cm.
Inflorescence: 50-150 cm.
Flowers: 35-45 mm.
Style: 7-10 mm.
Capsule: Small 35-50 mm, deeply constricted.
Distribution: USA (central Utah).
Altitude: 2400-2700 m.

▶ **Subsp. *kanabensis* (McKelvey) Hochstätter**
Synonyms: *Y. kanabensis* McKelvey; *Y. angustissima* var. *kanabensis* (McKelvey) Reveal.
Vernacular Name: Kanab Yucca.
Leaves: 45-75 cm.
Inflorescence: Over 2 m.
Flowers: 55-65 mm.
Style: 5-8 mm.
Capsule: Large 45-75 mm, somewhat constricted.

49b

49c

49d

Distribution: USA (south Utah, north Arizona).
Habitat: Sandy soil amongst sagebrush.
Altitude: 1300-2300 m.

Subsp. *toftiae* (Welsh) Hochstätter

Synonyms: *Y. toftiae* Welsh; *Y. angustissima* var. *toftiae* (Welsh) Reveal.
Vernacular Name: Toft Yucca.
Leaves: 25-60 cm.
Inflorescence: 1.5-4 m.
Flowers: 30-45 mm.
Style: 4-10 mm.
Capsule: Large 4.5-7.5 cm, somewhat constricted.
Distribution: USA (Utah, San Juan Co).

Yucca glauca Nuttall

Synonyms: *Y. angustifolia* Pursh, *Y. glauca* var. *rosea* D. M. Andrews.
Vernacular Name: Great Plains Yucca.
Habit: Stemless or with short stem of 0.5 m, producing either one rosette, or small to large confused clumps with many rosettes.
Leaves: Short, 25-45 cm, occasionally 60cm or more, moderately slender 0.7-1 cm, widest just beyond halfway, then tapering to terminal point, usually straight, mainly plano-convex, coarse, rather stiff, smooth on both surfaces, margins white or grey, sometimes with a few fine fibres.
Inflorescence: Usually simple raceme 0.4-1 m, very short scape, occasionally with a few branchlets.
Flowers: 46-61 mm long, greenish-cream, frequently tinged with rosy-brown, campanulate or extremely globose, with heavy fragrance.
Style: Ovoid, much enlarged near base, bright apple green.
Capsule: Small, usually 45-50 x 20 mm, stoutish, mainly symmetrical, occasionally constricted, obovoid or oblong-cylindrical, terminating in a beak.
Seeds: Over 12 mm, smooth, black, with a marginal wing.
Flowering: May-August.

This is another of the narrow leaf species, that is shy to flower. It seems to grow quite well outside here, though, and hardiness should not be a problem as it originates from areas where the winters are very harsh.

50a

49b *Y. angustissima* subsp. *avia,* nr Escalente, Utah
49c *Y. angustissima* subsp. *kanabensis,* nr Kanab, Utah
49d *Y. angusissima* subsp. *toftiae,* nr Hite, Utah
50a *Y. glauca*

▸ **Key to Subspecies**
1a. Leaves up to 75 cm long, inflorescence over 1.5 m   subsp. *stricta*
1b. Leaves 20-60 cm long, inflorescence up to 1 m   2

2a. Leaves 20-40 cm long, flowers white cream, capsule 40-60 x 10-15 mm   subsp. *albertana*
2b. Leaves 20-60 cm long, flowers white cream with pink brown stripes, capsule 50-100 x 20-30 mm   subsp. *glauca*

▸ Subsp. *glauca* Nuttall
Leaves: 20-60 cm.
Capsule: Up to 10 cm long.
Distribution: USA (Colorado, Iowa, Kansas, Missouri, Montana, Nebraska, New Mexico, North Dakota, Oklahoma, South Dakota, Wyoming).
Habitat: Plains, badlands and mountains.
Altitude: 800-2600 m.

▸ Subsp. *stricta* (Sims) Hochstätter.
Synonyms: *Y. glauca* var. *stricta* Sims; *Y. glauca* var. *gurneyi* McKelvey.
Vernacular Names: Small Soapweed Yucca.
Leaves: 75 cm.
Capsules: Up to 75 mm long.
Distribution: USA (northeast New Mexico, southeast Colorado, northwest Oklahoma, southwest Kansas).
Habitat: Mostly grassland.
Altitude: 900-500 m.

▸ Subsp. *albertana* Hochstätter
Vernacular Name: Palliser Triangle Yucca.
Leaves: 20-40 cm long, pale green.
Inflorescence: 40-80 cm.
Capsule: 40-60 x 10-15 mm long.
Distribution: Canada (southeast Alberta) USA (north Montana).

50b

Yucca baileyi Wooton and Standley

Synonyms: *Y. standleyi* McKelvey; *Y. navajou* Webber; *Y. baileyi* var. *navajou* Webber.
Vernacular Name: Alpine Yucca.
Habit: Plants normally stemless, occasionally may have a short upright stem and form a small clump with three to eighteen rosettes.
Leaves: 45 x 0.6 cm, linear, plano-convex, striate, pale green or yellow-green, margins white and finely filiferous.
Inflorescence: Simple raceme, 40-60 cm high, extending 5-20 cm above the foliage.
Flowers: 50-65 mm long, white to greenish-white.
Style: 7 mm, white, slender ovoid, slightly swollen toward base.
Capsule: 5-6 x 2.5 cm, oblong-cylindrical, not usually constricted.
Seeds: Thin, black with or without marginal wing.
Flowering: April-June.

The cold of a British winter should not be a problem for this plant because of the high altitude at which it grows. Here my plants have grown very well, but stubbornly refuse to flower. This plant is worth growing for the rosette of narrow leaves edged with curly filaments.

Key to Subspecies
1a. Leaves very filiferous, capsule up to 5 cm long   subsp. *baileyi*
1b. Leaves slightly filiferous, capsule up to 6 cm long
                                                        subsp. *intermedia*

Subsp. *baileyi* Wooton and Standley
Leaves: Strongly filiferous.
Flowers: Only when mature.
Capsule: Up to 5 cm long.
Distribution: USA (northern Arizona, northwest New Mexico, extreme southeast Utah).
Habitat: Thinly scattered in grassland and woodlands, on dry slopes.
Altitude: 1200-2600 m.

Subsp. *intermedia* (McKelvey) Hochstätter
Synonyms: *Y. intermedia* McKelvey; *Y. baileyi* var. *intermedia* (McKelvey) Reveal; *Y. intermedia* var. *ramosa* McKelvey.
Vernacular Name: Intermediate Yucca.
Leaves: Hardly filiferous.
Flowers: May occur before mature.
Capsule: To 6 cm long.

0b *Y. glauca* subsp. *stricta*
Y. baileyi, nr Bluff, Utah

Distribution: USA (central New Mexico).
Habitat: In different soils, often on the edge of juniper and pinyon pine woods.
Altitude: 1500-2000 m.

52a Y. whipplei, Arizona Sonora Desert Museum, Tucson, Arizona

Subgenus **Hesperoyucca** Engelmann

Yucca whipplei Torrey

Synonyms: *Y. californica* Groeland, *Y. graminifolia* Wood, *Hesperoyucca whipplei* (Torrey) Baker.
Vernacular Names: Our Lords Candle, Chaparral Yucca, Quichote Plant, Quixote Yucca.
Habit: Variable, from the monocarpic with a single rosette of leaves to clumps of many rosettes arising from offsets to clumps of scattered rosettes produced from suckers.
Leaves: 20-115 cm x 5-40 mm, tapering from base to apex, plano-convex or keeled on both surfaces, finely striate, rigid, sometimes glaucous, grey-green or less often yellow-green, purplish or brownish near tip, margins yellow, somewhat denticulate, terminal spine strong and sharp.
Inflorescence: 1.5-2.5 m, rarely to 4.5 m, scape variable, forming more or less than half the height, panicle cylindrical, slender-ellipsoidal or ovoid, dense-flowered.
Flowers: Variable, expanding broadly, or campanulate, 2-6.5 cm long, expanding broadly, greenish-white tinged with purple, margins sometimes brownish, fragrant.
Stigma: 3-lobed, covered in translucent glandular hairs, the overall shape being mushroom-like.
Style: Short and slender.
Capsule: 2-5 x 1.5-3 cm, obovoid or rounded to oblong, with short beak.
Seeds: 6-7 x 8 mm, flat, thin, smooth, dull black, without marginal wing.

This is one of the few self-fertile yuccas, which will set seed naturally in the UK.
J. Thiede in Eggli, ed., *Illustrated Handbook of Succulent Plants* (2001) considered this species so different from the rest of the genus that it should be put in a genus of its own. He therefore regarded *Hesperoyucca* Engelmann as a distinct genus, a view supported by recent molecular analysis by Bogler and Simpson (1995), Bogler and Simpson (1996) and Clary and Simpson (1995). However, it seems preferable to maintain a broad concept of *Yucca* as a whole.
In cultivation these plants require sheltered positions to survive and may take ten years or more to reach maturity and flowering. They require a deep root-run and therefore do not normally do well in

pots. In Cambridgeshire these plants all seem to limp along for a few years until death, although in a warmer microclimate they can be grown successfully.

The species is variable, and may be divided into six reasonably recognisable subspecies.

Key to Subspecies

1a. Rosettes solitary, monocarpic, dying after fruiting	2
1b. Rosettes forming groups, not monocarpic	3
2a. Rosettes spreading; in the juvenile stage the old, dry leaves are very persistent	subsp. *whipplei*
2b. Rosettes compact; in the juvenile stage the old dry leaves persist for a short time	subsp. *newberryi*
3a. New secondary rosettes formed from the base of the original rosette after flowering	4
3b. New rosettes arising on the rhizomes or leaf-axils prior to flowering	5
4a. Leaves narrow 0.7-2 cm and flexible	subsp. *intermedia*
4b. Leaves broad, 2-4 cm, stiff, sword-like leaves	subsp. *eremica*
5a. Plant forming dense cushions producing several inflorescences in spring; secondary rosettes produced form leaf-axils	subsp. *caespitosa*
5b. Plants forming large, open mats, producing one inflorescence in spring; secondary rosettes from rhizomes	subsp. *percursa*

Subsp. *whipplei* Torrey

Habit: monocarpic with single rosette of spreading leaves (even in juvenile stage).

Leaves: 25-115 x 0.5-3.3 cm, tapering from widest point at union with base to apex, plano-convex, or keeled on both surfaces, finely striate, rigid, sometimes glaucous, grey-green or less often yellow-green, purplish near tip, margins yellow, somewhat denticulate, terminal spine strong and sharp, old leaves persistent.

Inflorescence: 80-250 cm, rarely to 450 cm; scape variable forming more or less half the height, panicle cylindrical or slender-ellipsoidal, dense.

Ovary: 7-13 mm, stout, obovoid, somewhat depressed at top, 6-lobed with rather deep fissures, each lobe round-backed.

Style: 1.6-3.2 mm, slender and white.

Capsule: 3-5 x 1.5-3 cm, obovoid with short beak, opening loculicidally.

Seed: 6-7 x 8 mm, flat, thin, smooth, dull to glossy, black, without marginal wing.

Flowering: March-May.

52b *Y. whipplei* subsp. *eremica*

Distribution: USA (southern California, San Diego area, Orange, Riverside, San Bernadino, Los Angeles, Ventura, Santa Barbara, Kern, San Luis, Obispo and Tulare Counties, south central Monterey and south east San Benito Counties).
Habitat: Dry grassy hills and chaparral.
Altitude: 600-1500 m.

Subsp. *caespitosa* (Jones) Haines

Synonym: *Y. whipplei* var. *caespitosa* Jones.
Habit: stemless, tufted, forming large dense clumps of over 100 rosettes.
Leaves: 20-50 x 1-2 cm.
Inflorescence: 1.5-3 m, cylindrical to ellipsoid.
Flowers: 2-3 cm.
Style: 4 mm.
Capsule: 2-3 x 2-3 cm, rounded.
Distribution: USA (South California, San Bernardino and Kern Counties, south and west facing slopes of the Mojave Desert.
Habitat: Open juniper woods and desert scrub.
Altitude: 500-1200 m.

Subsp. *eremica* Epling and Haines

Synonym: *Y. peninsularis* McKelvey.

Habit: Stemless, solitary or forming small clumps.
Leaves: 20-40 x 2-4 cm, narrowing from base to apex, terminal spine brownish, and very strong.
Inflorescence: 1.5-2.5 m.
Capsule: 2-4 cm, round to oblong, capsule woodier and stronger than in other subspecies.
Seed: 6-8 x 6-8 x 1 mm.
Flowering: April-May.
Distribution: Mexico (North Baja, California).
Habitat: Flat ground or steep ridges.
Altitude: 300-750 m.

Subsp. *intermedia* Haines

Synonym: *Y. whipplei* var. *intermedia* (Haines) Webber.
Habit: Stemless, forming groups of a few rosettes; new rosettes

developing around base of the dying rosette after flowering.
Leaves: 25-80 cm long, narrow (7-20 mm) and flexible.
Inflorescence: 1-2.5 m.
Distribution: USA (California, Santa Monica and Santa Susana mountains, Los Angeles and Ventura counties).
Altitude: Sea level-600 m.

Subsp. *newberryi* (McKelvey) Hochstätter
Synonym: *Y. newberryi* McKelvey.
Habit: Stemless, rosettes solitary, monocarpic, compact when juvenile.
Leaves: 20-60 cm, the old dry leaves persist for only a short time.
Inflorescence: 2-3 m panicle, ovoid.
Flowers: 3.5 cm.
Capsule: 2 x 2 cm.
Distribution: USA (Arizona, south rim of Colorado River, Mohave County).
Altitude: 400-1300 m.

Subsp. *percursa* Haines
Synonym: *Y. whipplei* var. *percursa* (Haines) Webber.
Habit: Forming clumps derived from rhizomes, spreading over a wide area to produce scattered mats.
Leaves: 20-40 cm, greenish, rather rigid.
Flowers: 1-3 cm, campanulate, white, often with brown margins.
Capsule: 2-3 x 2-3 cm.
Distribution: USA (California, Cochuma and San Rafael Mountains, Santa Barbara County).
Habitat: Mountain ridges and mesas in coastal sagebrush and chaparral.
Altitude: Sea level-600 m.

a

b

c

Hybrids

There have been over 100 true artificial yucca hybrids (i.e. developed by crossing various species). The majority of these were developed at the turn of last century. Some never became commercially available, and many others were lost to cultivation during the two World Wars, although it is possible that some have survived unrecognised.

I am only aware of four hybrids currently commercially available; therefore I shall restrict my descriptions to these, detailed below. Please see also Appendix II for further details of prominent breeders and their full hybrid lists.

Yucca × *floribunda* Sprenger (1903)

Habit: Forms a clump, may produce many stems.
Leaves: Large without filaments.
Flowers: Abundant, waxy-white. (A very floriferous form)

This hybrid was developed by Carlo Sprenger, by crossing *Y. filamentosa* and *Y. gloriosa,* although Professor G. Molon thought it more likely to be between *Y. flaccida* and *Y. recurvifolia*. It is unusual in that it will do well in some shade.

This hybrid should not be confused with one of the same name produced by J. R. Deleuil that differs in producing a large trunk and leaves, dark green, rigid, pleated.

Yucca × *karlsruhensis* Graebner (1899)

Habit: Plants without stems.
Leaves: Long, linear, greyish-green.
Inflorescence: Panicle to 1.5 m.
Flowers: Large predominantly white.

P. Graebner made this hybrid between *Y. filamentosa* and *Y. glauca*.

Yucca 'Vittorio Emanuele II' Sprenger (1901)

Habit: Plant produces trunk with upright branches.
Leaves: Numerous, long, start erect and become inclined, glaucous.
Inflorescence: Enormous, up to 2 m.
Flowers: Carmine in bud, opening to large campanulate bells, interior sugary-white.

Carlo Sprenger produced this plant from *Y. recurvifolia* and *Y. aloifolia* forma *purpurea*.

Yucca × *vomerensis* Sprenger (1901)

Habit: Produce a somewhat elevated trunk.
Leaves: Numerous, start erect but with time become more inclined, eventually assume a pendula posture, leaves pleated glaucous-green.
Inflorescence: Large 2.2-2.5 m high.

Hybrids
a *Y.* × *karlsruhensis*
b *Y.* × *floribunda*
c *Y.* 'Vittorio Emanuele II'
d *Y.* × *vomerensis*

d

Flowers: Large, open, greenish-white, suffused red-brown externally.

Another Carlo Sprenger hybrid, formed from *Y. aloifolia* and *Y. gloriosa,* although in Professor Molon's opinion the parents were more likely to have been *Y. aloifolia* and *Y. recurvifolia.* This plant has the characteristics of the parents.

Appendix I

Plants considered hardy in the United Kingdom.

Yucca angustissima — *Yucca angustissima* subsp. *kanabensis*
Yucca arkansana — *Yucca baccata*
Yucca baileyi — *Yucca baileyi* subsp. *intermedia*
Yucca campestris — *Yucca carnerosana*
Yucca faxoniana — *Yucca flaccida* and cultivars
Yucca filifera — *Yucca filamentosa* (except forma *variegata*)
Yucca glauca — *Yucca gloriosa* and cultivars
Yucca recurvifolia and cultivars — *Yucca schottii*

Plants which are not hardy but are suitable for pots.

Yucca aloifolia — *Yucca arizonica*
Yucca elephantipes — *Yucca rostrata*
Yucca thompsoniana — *Yucca torreyi*
Yucca treculeana

Plants only suitable for planting in a greenhouse, as they are not hardy enough to grow outside and require a deep root run.

Yucca brevifolia — *Yucca elata*

Appendix II

Breeders and cultivars

J. B. Deleuil: based himself initially at Marseilles in 1874, later moving along the coast to Hyeres in 1902. He produced some 3000 plants, of which some hybrids were named.

Yucca 'Andreana'	*Yucca* 'Carrierei'	*Yucca* 'Deleuili'
Yucca × *dracaenoides*	*Yucca* × *ensifera*	*Yucca* × *floribunda*
Yucca × *juncea*	*Yucca* × *gracillima*	*Yucca* × *laevigata*
Yucca 'Lucida'	*Yucca* 'Messiliensis'	*Yucca* × *pilosa*
Yucca × *procera*	*Yucca* × *striatula*	*Yucca* × *sulcata*

Graebner: based at Corte, Corsica. He produced.
Yucca x *karlsruhensis* (1903)
Yucca 'Graebneri' (A sport of the above)

Carlo Sprenger: based at Vomero near Naples from 1899 onwards, produced a large number of hybrids and cultivars, many of which never became available to the public.

Yucca 'Ada'	*Yucca* × *adenophora*	*Yucca* 'Albella'
Yucca 'Altroides'	*Yucca* 'Alexandrae'	*Yucca* × *amabilis*
Yucca × *amoena*	*Yucca* 'Arnottiana'	*Yucca* 'Atropos'
Yucca 'Augusta'	*Yucca* 'Aurora'	*Yucca* 'Casertana'
Yucca 'Ceres'	*Yucca* × *chinensis*	*Yucca* 'Clotho'
Yucca × *coelestis*	*Yucca* 'Colombiana'	*Yucca* × *columnaris*
Yucca 'Darwinii'	*Yucca* 'Diana'	*Yucca* 'Draco'
Yucca × *dux*	*Yucca* × *elegantissima*	*Yucca* × *elmensis*
Yucca 'Elwesiana'	*Yucca* 'Engelmannii'	*Yucca* × *ensata*
Yucca 'Eros'	*Yucca* 'Europa'	*Yucca* × *exsultans*
Yucca 'Fredericus Caesar'	*Yucca filamentosa nobilis*	
Yucca filamentosa voluntaria	*Yucca* 'Flora'	*Yucca* × *floribunda*
Yucca × *formosa*	*Yucca* 'Fosteriana'	*Yucca* 'Gaea'
Yucca × *grandis*	*Yucca* 'Guglielmi'	*Yucca* 'Heliodorus'
Yucca 'Helios'	*Yucca* × *imperator*	*Yucca* × *imperialis*
Yucca 'Ismene'	*Yucca* 'Koelliana'	*Yucca* 'Lachesis'
Yucca × *lanceolata*		
Yucca × *lawrenceana*	*Yucca* × *liliacea*	*Yucca* 'Luna'
Yucca × *luxurians*	*Yucca* × *magnifica*	*Yucca* × *magnolia*
Yucca × *margaritacea*	*Yucca* 'Mariae'	*Yucca* × *micans*
Yucca 'Minerva'	*Yucca* 'Moraea'	*Yucca* 'Nicotrana'

Yucca 'Oceanus'	*Yucca* × *paradoxa*	*Yucca* 'Partenope'
Yucca 'Passiflora'	*Yucca* 'Peregrina'	*Yucca* 'Praecox'
Yucca × *princeps*	*Yucca* 'Psyche'	*Yucca* × *purpurescens*
Yucca × *regalis*	*Yucca* 'Rekowskiana'	*Yucca* × *rex*
Yucca × *robusta*	*Yucca* 'Sanderiana'	*Yucca* 'Saturnus'
Yucca 'Sieheana'	*Yucca* 'Smaragdina'	*Yucca* 'Sokrates'
Yucca 'Titanus'	*Yucca* 'Treleasii'	*Yucca* 'Triton'
Yucca × *tulipifera*	*Yucca* × *viridiflora*	
Yucca 'Vittorio Emanuele II'	*Yucca* × *virescens*	*Yucca* 'Virgilius'
Yucca × *vomerensis*	*Yucca* 'Washington'	
Yucca 'Willmottiana'	*Yucca* 'Wittmachiana'	

Willy Müller: worked for Carlo Sprenger for fourteen years, then purchased from him the entire collection and transported it to his own nursery nearby. From 1908 onwards he offered these hybrids.

Yucca 'Sprengerii' *Yucca* 'Moloniana'
Yucca 'Williamsiana'

He also produced several of his own hybrids of his own, none of which were named.

Karl Foerster: based at Potsdam-Bornim, near Berlin. From about 1930 to 1935 he worked at a state-run nursery near Potsdam and carried out experimental work on fibre extraction from yucca leaves. Karl Foerster was able to select the best plants from the thousands at the trial site. For the next thirty years, these selected forms of *Yucca filamentosa* were kept going by his nursery foreman, Paul Bolz. In 1967 he was finally able to launch his catalogue, containing five yucca varieties. Sadly he died in 1970, the management of the nursery passing to Dr. Konrad Nässer. Subsequent catalogues contained two further varieties, in addition to which there was also an unofficial list of named varieties, which had found its way to other nurseries. From various sources I have compiled the following:

Yucca filamentosa 'Atlanta'

Yucca filamentosa Bornimer Auswahlmischung
(This was not a single variety but a collection of plants that were considered better than the average.)

Yucca filamentosa 'Eisbär' *Yucca filamentosa* 'Elegantissima'

Yucca filamentosa 'Elite' *Yucca filamentosa* 'Florida'

Yucca filamentosa 'Fontäne' *Yucca filamentosa* 'Glockenriese'

Yucca filamentosa 'Grossglockner' *Yucca filamentosa* 'Herkulessaule'

Yucca filamentosa 'Missouri' *Yucca filamentosa* 'Rosenglocke'

Yucca filamentosa 'Schellenbaum' *Yucca filamentosa* 'Schneefichte'

Yucca filamentosa 'Schneetanne' *Yucca filamentosa* 'St. Louis'

Professor F.N. Rusanov: was the Director at the Botanical Institute and Botanical Garden in Tashkent, Republic of Uzbekistan. He created over 150 hybrids, including extending the colour range by intensifying the red colouration. Unfortunately none seem to have reached the United Kingdom so far.

Appendix III

Where to obtain Yuccas

Most garden centres carry a small selection of yucca but to obtain some of the more unusual plants, a visit to a more specialist nursery would be required. These are listed in the R.H.S. *Plant Finder* published by Dorling Kindersley.

To obtain seed of the more unusual yuccas try:

Mesa Garden, PO Box 72, Belen, N M 87002, USA.

Navajo Country, P.O. Box 510201, D-68242 Mannheim, Germany.

Where to see Yuccas

In the United Kingdom:

C. Smith, Spring View, 10 Spring Close, Burwell, Cambridge CB50HF. Telephone 01638 742993 *Open by appointment*

T. Key, 15 Newbold Avenue, Newbold, Chesterfield, Derbyshire S41 7AR. Telephone 01246 237178
(The collection however is at Renishaw Hall, Eckington, nr Sheffield)

The Royal Botanic Gardens, Kew, Richmond, Surrey. Telephone 01819401171

In Europe:

Hanbury Botanical Garden, La Mortola, Cape Mortola, Ventimiglia, Italy. Telephone 00 39 184 229 507

Villa Thuret. Boulevard du Cape d' Antibes, France. Telephone 00 33 93 678866

Jardin Exotique Eze, Rue du Chateau, 06620 Eze, France.

Jardín Botánico Tropical, Pinya de Rosa, Sta. Cristina, Blanes, Spain.

Jardí Botánic, Marimurtra, Blanes, Spain. Telephone 00 34 972 33 0826

In USA

Desert Botanical Garden, 1201 N. Galvin Parkway, Phoenix, AZ 85008. Telephone 480-941-1225

Boyce Thompson Arboretum, 37615 Hwy. 60 superior, AZ 85273. Telephone 520-689-2811

Arizona-Sonora Desert Museum 2021 N. Kinney Road, Tucson, AZ 85743. Telephone 520-883-2702

Appendix IV

Glossary

Attenuate	tapering
Beak	pointed like the bill of a bird
Capitate	head like structure
Campanulate	bell shaped
Concavo-convex	hollowed out on top curved down underneath
Cylindrical	a straight roller shaped body
Dehiscent	seed capsules that burst open
Denticulate	with very small teeth
Ellipsoidal	a solid with oval shape profile
Filiferous	having thread like structures
Flocculate	woolly
Glabrous	smooth, without hairs
Globose	spherical
Indehiscent	capsules not splitting to release seeds
Inflorescence	arrangement of flowers upon a stem
Lanceolate	curved sides tapering to a point at either end
Ligulate	tongue shaped
Linear	slender and narrow
Loculicidal	splitting side of the chamber to release seed
Monocarpic	dying after fruiting
Obovoid	egg shaped with widest part at the extremity
Obpyriform	pear shaped with narrowest section at the extremity
Panicle	flowers arranged on a multi-branched structure
Pedicel	the stalk that supports a single flower
Perianth	showy portion of flower consisting of petals and sepals
Plano-convex	flat on top curved underneath in profile
Polymorphic	having many shapes
Prismatic	having several longitudinal angles and flat surfaces between
Pubescent	downy with short soft hairs
Raceme	flowers arranged up a central stalk
Scape	the shaft that holds the flower bearing structure
Septicidal	capsule splitting along internal wall to release seed
Spatulate	broad knife shape
Stigma	part of pistil that receives the pollen
Striate	marked with thin lines, grooves or ridges
Style	the prolongation from ovary that carries the stigma
Tepal	a sepal that has developed to take the form of a petal
Undulate	having a wave like surface

Bibliography

CLARY K. H. (1995), *Yucca linearifolia*: A new, indehiscent, fleshy-fruited, linear-leaved species endemic to the Chihuahuan Desert, Mexico. Brittonia, 47(4), pp. 394-396.
CORRELL D. S. and JOHNSTON M. C. (1979), Manual of the vascular plants of Texas. Texas Research Foundation, pp. 395-402.
FERNALD M. L. (1944), Rhodora, 46, New England Botanical Club, pp. 8-9
IRISH M. and G. (2000), Agaves, Yuccas and Related Plants. Timber Press.
HOCHSTÄTTER F. (2000), Yucca I. in the Southwest and Midwest of the USA and Canada. Published by the author.
HOCHSTÄTTER F. (2002), Yucca II. Published by the author.
HYAMS E. and MACQUITTY W. (1985), Great Botanical Gardens of the World. Bloomsbury Books.
KEARNEY T. H. and PEEBLES R. H. (1951), The Flora of Arizona. University of California Press, pp. 185-188.
KEITH E.L. (2003), *Yucca cernua* (Agavaceae: Series rupicolae), a new species from Newton and Jasper Counties in eastern Texas. SIDA 20(3), pp.891-898.
LAFERRIÈRE J.E. (1995), *Yucca declinata*: a new species from the Sonora. Cactus and Succulent Journal (U.S.), Vol.67, pp.347-348.
LENZ L. W. (1998), *Yucca capensis*. A new species from Baja California Sur Mexico, Cactus and Succulent Journal (U.S.) Vol 70, No. 6, pp.289-296.
LUJÁN I. P. (1989), Una nueva espicie del Genero Yucca, Cact. Suc. Mex. 34, pp. 51-56.
LUJÁN I.P. (1990), Nuevas aportacions a *Yucca queretaroensis*, Cact. Suc. Mex. 35, pp. 61-62.
MATUDA S.D. and LUJÁN I.P. (1980), Las Plantas Mexicanas del Genero Yucca, Mescelanea Estado De Mexico.
MCKELVEY S.D. (1938) Yuccas of the southwestern United States, part 1, The Arnold Arboretum of Harvard University.
MCKELVEY S. D. (1947) Yuccas of the southwestern United States, part 2, The Arnold Arboretum of Harvard University.
MITCH L. W. (1977) Uses of the Genus Yucca, Excelsa No. 7 pp.45-56.
MOLON G. (1914) Le Yucche, Ulrico Hoepli Editore Libraio Della Real Casa, Milano.
MUNZ P. A. (1959) A California Flora, University of California Press, pp. 1360-1363.

THIEDE J. (2001) Agavaceae. In Egli U. (ed.) Illustrated Handbook of Succulent Plants (Monocotyledons).
TRELEASE W. (1902) The Yuccaceae, Rep. Miss. Bot. Gard. Vol. 13, pp. 27-133.
TRELEASE W. (1907) Additions To The Genus Yucca, Rep. Miss. Bot. Gard. Vol. 18, pp. 225-230.
TRELEASE W. (1911) An Additional Tree Yucca And One Other Species New In The United States, Rep. Miss. Bot. Gard. Vol. 22, pp.101-103.
WEBBER J. M. (1953) Yuccas Of The Southwest, U. S. D. A. Monograph 17, pp. 1-65.
WELSH S.L. (1977) Reveal Intermount Fl. 6, pp527-536.

Index

Clistoyucca arborescens	31
Hesperoyucca whipplei	57
Samuela carnerosana	16
Samuela faxoniana	17
Yucca aloifolia	5, 11, 23, **24**, 62
Yucca aloifolia forma *marginata*	**24**, 25
Yucca aloifolia forma *medio-picta*	25
Yucca aloifolia forma *tricolor*	**24**, 25
Yucca aloifolia forma *variegata*	25
Yucca aloifolia var. *yucatana*	24
Yucca angustifolia	47, 53
Yucca angustifolia var. *mollis*	44
Yucca angustissima	33, **51**
Yucca angustissima subsp. *angustissima*	51
Yucca angustissima subsp. *avia*	51, **52**
Yucca angustissima var. *avia*	52
Yucca angustissima subsp. *kanabensis*	51, **52**
Yucca angustissima var. *kanabensis*	52
Yucca angustissima subsp. *toftiae*	51, **52**, 53
Yucca angustissima var. *toftiae*	53
Yucca arborescens	31
Yucca arizonica	10, 13, **14**
Yucca arkansana	33, **44**
Yucca arkansana subsp. *arkansana*	44, **45**
Yucca arkansana subsp. *freemanii*	44, **45**
Yucca arkansana subsp. *louisanensis*	44, **45**
Yucca arkansana var. *paniculata*	45
Yucca australis	17, 22
Yucca baccata	5, 6, 10, **12**, 13, 18
Yucca baccata subsp. *australis*	22
Yucca baccata subsp. *baccata*	12
Yucca baccata var. *macrocarpa*	14
Yucca baccata subsp. *thornberi*	13
Yucca baccata subsp. *vespertina*	**12**, 13
Yucca baccata var. *vespertina*	13
Yucca baileyi	33, **55**
Yucca baileyi subsp. *baileyi*	55
Yucca baileyi subsp. *intermedia*	55
Yucca baileyi var. *intermedia*	55
Yucca baileyi var. *navajou*	55
Yucca brevifolia	31
Yucca brevifolia subsp. *brevifolia*	32
Yucca brevifolia forma *herbertii*	32
Yucca brevifolia subsp. *herbertii*	**32**
Yucca brevifolia var. *herbertii*	32
Yucca brevifolia subsp. *jaegeriana*	**32**
Yucca brevifolia var. *jaegeriana*	32
Yucca brevifolia var. *wolfei*	32
Yucca californica	57
Yucca campestris	33, **46**
Yucca capensis	11, 28
Yucca canaliculata	19
Yucca carnerosana	7, 10, **16**
Yucca cernua	33, 37
Yucca coahuilensis	33, **46**
Yucca colo-ma	49
Yucca concava	38, 40
Yucca confinis	13
Yucca constricta	33, **43**
Yucca crenulata	24
Yucca decipiens	11, **20**
Yucca declinata	11, 22
Yucca desmetiana	11, **23**
Yucca draconis	24
Yucca elata	5, 6, 18, 33, **47**
Yucca elata subsp. *elata*	**47**
Yucca elata subsp. *utahensis*	47, **48**
Yucca elata var. *utahensis*	48
Yucca elata subsp. *verdiensis*	47, **48**
Yucca elata var. *verdiensis*	48
Yucca elephantipes	6, 7, 8, 11, 18, **28**
Yucca elephantipes 'Head Jewel'	**29**
Yucca elephantipes 'Jewel'	**29**
Yucca elephantipes 'Puck'	**29**
Yucca elephantipes 'Silver Star'	**29**
Yucca endlichiana	10, 17
Yucca faxoniana	10 16, **17**
Yucca filamentosa	33, 38, **39**, 42
Yucca filamentosa 'Bright Edge'	**39**, 40
Yucca filamentosa 'Color Guard'	**40**
Yucca filamentosa subsp. *concava*	39, 40
Yucca filamentosa 'Eisbär'	40
Yucca filamentosa 'Elegantissima'	41
Yucca filamentosa subsp. *filamentosa*	39
Yucca filamentosa 'Glockenriese'	**40**, 41
Yucca filamentosa 'Gilt Edge'	**40**, 41
Yucca filamentosa 'Rosenglocke'	**41**
Yucca filamentosa 'Schellenbaum'	**41**
Yucca filamentosa 'Schneefichte'	**41**
Yucca filamentosa 'Schneetanne'	**41**, 42
Yucca filamentosa subsp. *smalliana*	39
Yucca filamentosa forma *variegata*	42
Yucca filifera	7, 11, **22**
Yucca flaccida	33, **42**

Yucca flaccida 'Golden Sword' 42, **43**
Yucca flaccida 'Ivory' **43**
Yucca flaccida striated cultivar **43**
Yucca flexilis 11, 27
Yucca × *floribunda* 7, **60**, 61
Yucca freemanii 45
Yucca gilbertiana 50
Yucca glauca 5, 33, **53**
Yucca glauca subsp. *albertana* 54
Yucca glauca subsp. *glauca* 54
Yucca glauca var. *gurneyi* 54
Yucca glauca mollis 44
Yucca glauca var. *rosea* 53
Yucca glauca subsp. *stricta* 54, **55**
Yucca glauca var. *stricta* 54
Yucca gloriosa 5, 7, 11, 25, **26**, 27, 62
Yucca gloriosa 'Ellacombei' 26
Yucca gloriosa forma *marginata* **26**
Yucca gloriosa forma *nobilis* **26**
Yucca gloriosa forma *variegata* **26**
Yucca graminifolia 57
Yucca grandiflora 10, **15**
Yucca guatamalensis 28
Yucca harrimaniae 33, **49**, 50
Yucca harrimaniae subsp. *gilbertiana* 9, 49, **50**
Yucca harrimaniae var. *gilbertiana* 50
Yucca harrimaniae subsp. *harrimaniae* 49, 50
Yucca harrimaniae subsp. *neomexicana* 9, 49, **50**
Yucca harrimaniae var. *neomexicana* 50
Yucca harrimaniae subsp. *sterilis* 49, 50
Yucca harrimaniae var. *sterilis* 50
Yucca intermedia 55
Yucca intermedia var. *ramosa* 55
Yucca jaliscensis 11, **21**
Yucca kanabensis 52
Yucca × *karlsruhensis* **60**, 61
Yucca lacandonica 11, **30**
Yucca linearifolia 11, **25**
Yucca louisianensis 43, 45
Yucca macrocarpa 14, 15
Yucca madrensis 11, 18, **30**
Yucca mixtecana 10, 19
Yucca mohavensis 15
Yucca nana 33, **48**
Yucca navajou 55
Yucca necopina 33, 45

Yucca neomexicana 50
Yucca newberryi 60
Yucca pallida 33, **37**, 45
Yucca pendula 27
Yucca peninsularis 59
Yucca periculosa 11, **21**
Yucca potosina 11, **23**
Yucca queretaroensis 33, **34**
Yucca radiosa 47
Yucca recurva 27
Yucca recurvifolia 5, 7, 11, **27**, 62
Yucca recurvifolia forma *marginata* **27**, 28
Yucca recurvifolia forma *variegata* **27**, 28
Yucca reverchoni 33, **36**
Yucca rigida 33, **35**
Yucca rostrata 33, **36**
Yucca rostrata forma *integra* 36
Yucca rupicola 9, 33, 36, **38**
Yucca rupicola var. *rigida* 34, 35
Yucca rupicola var. *tortifolia* 38
Yucca schidigera 10, **15**
Yucca schottii 7, 10, **18**
Yucca schottii var. *jaliscensis* 21
Yucca smalliana 38, 39
Yucca standleyi 55
Yucca tenuistyla 43
Yucca thompsoniana 5, 33, 34, **35**
Yucca thornberi 10, **13**
Yucca toftiae 53
Yucca torreyi 5, 6, 10, **14**
Yucca torreyi forma *parviflora* 14
Yucca treculeana 10, **19**
Yucca utahensis 48
Yucca valida 11, **20**
Yucca verdiensis 48
Yucca vespertina 13
Yucca 'Vittorio Emanuele II' **60**, 61
Yucca × *vomerensis* **61**
Yucca whipplei **56**, 57
Yucca whipplei subsp. *caespitosa* 58, 59
Yucca whipplei var. *caespitosa* 59
Yucca whipplei subsp. *eremica* 58, **59**
Yucca whipplei subsp. *intermedia* 58, 59
Yucca whipplei var. *intermedia* 59
Yucca whipplei subsp. *newberryi* 58, 60
Yucca whipplei subsp. *percursa* 58, 60
Yucca whipplei var. *percursa* 60
Yucca whipplei subsp. *whipplei* 58
Yucca yucatana 24